W9-ARH-135

did
u

know

What they didn't teach you in photo school

what you actually
need to know
to succeed
in this industry

DEMETRIUS
FORDHAM

ilex

What They Didn't Teach You in Photo School

An Hachette UK Company
www.hachette.co.uk

First published in Great Britain in 2015 by ILEX,
a division of Octopus Publishing Group Ltd
Octopus Publishing Group
Carmelite House
50 Victoria Embankment
London, EC4Y 0DZ
www.octopusbooks.co.uk

Design, layout, and text copyright
© Octopus Publishing Group 2015

Distributed in the US by Hachette Book Group
1290 Avenue of the Americas, 45th and 5th Floors
New York, NY 10020

Distributed in Canada by Canadian Manda Group
664 Annette St., Toronto, Ontario, Canada M6S 2C8

Executive Publisher: Roly Allen
Senior Specialist Editor: Frank Gallaugher
Senior Project Editor: Natalia Price-Cabrera
Assistant Editor: Rachel Silverlight
Associate Publisher: Adam Juniper
Art Director: Julie Weir
Designer: Simon Goggin
Senior Production Manager: Peter Hunt

All rights reserved. No part of this work may be reproduced
or utilized in any form or by any means, electronic or mechanical,
including photocopying, recording or by any information storage
and retrieval system, without the prior written permission of
the publisher.

ISBN 978-1-78157-269-6

A CIP catalogue record for this book is available from the British Library

Printed and bound in China

10 9 8 7 6 5 4

CONTENTS

INTRODUCTION

Though many working photographers have argued otherwise, traditional photography schools are not irrelevant or obsolete. Despite their curricular limitations, the majority of photo schools still offer a good introduction to the industry and equip students with the fundamental technical skills required for professional photography.

But it is not enough. Though photo school can offer a rudimentary educational foundation for aspiring photographers, it fails to teach the kind of raw, practical, real-world lessons and advice necessary to navigate, survive, and succeed in today's complex, fast-paced, and absurdly competitive industry.

Thanks to technology and the internet, there have never been more working photographers across the world than there are today. Statistics simultaneously reveal that it's never been harder to make a living at this. You must not only be skilled at his or her craft, but must also be a marketing whiz, social-media extraordinaire, avid blogger, website expert, and entrepreneur in order to flourish. On top of all this, you are required to be financially literate, business-savvy, and unfailingly professional while confronting continual critique and rejection. Historically, there's never been a more difficult or complicated time to be a photographer—yet one can also argue that it's never been so rewarding, either.

All that in mind, this book was written by a working, modern-day photographer with the humble intention of helping fellow working, modern-day photographers "figure it all out." The information, lessons, and advice within these pages are rooted in the real-world experiences (and mistakes) of many accomplished photographers, photo assistants, and industry professionals. Like the title suggests, it aims to offer the kind of practical, unfiltered advice that they "didn't teach you in photo school," from step-by-step breakdowns on what to really expect on a photo shoot, to handling finances and trying to run a profitable business. While it aims to be something of an insider's guide to working in the profession, it cannot possibly encapsulate everything there is to know about being a photographer in today's industry.

For more resources, including downloadable model-release forms, sample invoices, and other paperwork templates, check out www.ilexinstant.com/resources.

Rewarding

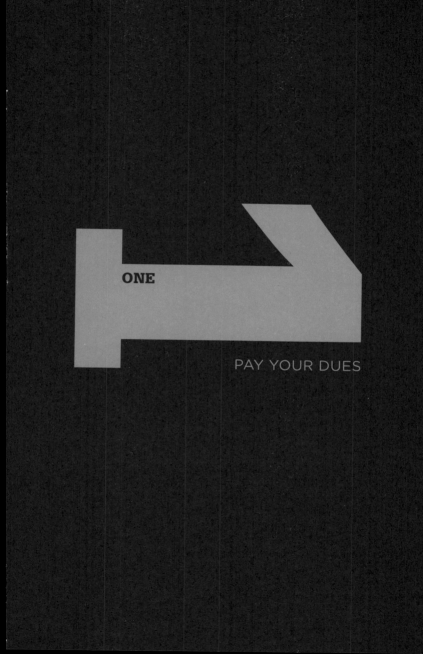

ONE

PAY YOUR DUES

So, you just graduated from photo school, you know how to use a camera and frame a shot, and you're ready to start shooting some editorials and ad campaigns! Though the enthusiasm is great—hang onto it—the reality is that, like with any career, you're going to have to start at the bottom and work your way up to the top.

Author Note
All of this might sound intimidating, but this is when your real education kicks off. Every successful photographer started where you are now, so approach your work, paid or not, with eagerness and a willingness to learn. You might have just finished photo school but the truth is, you're just at the beginning.

You'll most likely be cutting your teeth on other photographers' sets before running your own. Instead of taking pictures, you'll be taking equipment orders, unloading grip trucks, setting up lights, and holding up reflectors. Though the pictures you see in magazines and on billboards might look effortless, glamorous, and easy, the process of making them is not. For a while, you might even have to work for free.

You also need to get real-world education on the wider industry into which you've just entered. Photo school might have taught you how to navigate a set, but navigating the competitive, cutthroat world of professional photography? That's another thing entirely. Like with any profession, skills simply don't cut it; you need to be an expert in your industry and understand how it works. This means active study, attending industry events and seminars, and seeking mentorship (more on all that later).

START FROM THE BOTTOM

Unless you are incredibly lucky or supernaturally talented, your first time on a production set or handling high-end photography equipment will be in a volunteering or assisting capacity. Embrace it, because this initial "supporting role" is a good thing—you'll need to learn the ropes before you can run the show. Here, you'll apply the basic technical skills you learned in photo school and learn from any mistakes you make.

VOLUNTEERING & INTERNING

As a volunteer or intern, you have the opportunity to familiarize yourself with professional photography gear and put your technical skills to good use with little pressure or responsibility. There are two main places you can do this:

Equipment rental houses: Processing orders in the equipment room of a large photography rental house is one of the best ways to get acquainted with the cameras, lighting, and digital gear used on working sets. You'll quickly learn what equipment is required for different productions, while mingling and networking with others in the industry (mainly assistants in charge of pick-ups and other production staff). Cool bonus: You'll be the first to get your hands on the latest camera models.

Attitude

"When you're just starting out in the industry, jump on any opportunity to be around a real-world production environment. Interning at a photo studio, in particular, allows you to witness photographers on set with clients and a production crew, and watch actual work unfold. Don't take it for granted, soak in everything you can. It's an excellent learning experience and step in the door."

PETER CLARK
OWNER, NEW YORK CITY'S ATTIC STUDIOS

Author Note
Assisting or "teching" is a great way of supporting yourself while pursuing your own photography career. It's often the bread and butter of aspiring and emerging photographers who want to work in the industry while building their own portfolios, networking, and honing their technical skills. I worked for seven years as a photo assistant before being able to support myself shooting full time.

Photography studios: Unless a photography studio has its own equipment room (smaller studios generally don't), you won't get your claws on as many cool cameras or gear as you would working at a rental house. That said, you do get the opportunity to lend a hand during real-world productions and watch assistants, digital techs, and photographers at work. You may not be getting paid for your efforts, but still act as if you are. Making a good impression on these people has a greater impact than you could imagine.

PHOTO ASSISTING

Being a photographer's assistant is a step up from interning or volunteering at a rental house or studio. In this role, you'll work alongside a photographer during the shoot itself (as well as before and after it, in various pre- and post-production tasks) and will own many responsibilities. These can range from handling and organizing equipment, to managing the precious digital assets of a shoot. Unlike an intern or volunteer, you are integral to the success of a production—without you, the photographer might not be able to adequately perform his or her services—and so this will always be a paid role.

Assistant

Photo assisting is the best way to learn on-set jargon, the shoot anatomy, industry politics, and the overall business of photography, all while rubbing shoulders with actual clients, producers, creative directors, assistants, and stylists. It has also been a rite of passage for many famous photographers and is considered an excellent pathway to the profession.

GET AN INDUSTRY EDUCATION

Though interning, volunteering, and photo assisting give you on-the-job experience and allow you to hone and perfect your technical skills, experience and abilities won't go far if you don't have an understanding of the wider industry you work in. Photo school may have taught you a general overview of the modern-day photo industry, but navigating it and trying to work within it are something else entirely. As an emerging professional photographer, you should continuously educate yourself on the industry that you're a part of: how it operates, how it's changed and how it's changing, its issues, and its key players. Like with any profession, you should be an expert at both the craft itself and the wider field in which you work.

"I think the lone-wolf mentality that photographers have has not been good for the profession. I recommend joining a photo organization. They have done a ton of good over the years, and the more people get involved, the more they can advocate for photographers."

ROB HAGGART
FORMER PHOTO EDITOR & FOUNDER, APHOTOEDITOR.COM

RESEARCH KEY PLAYERS

Do some research to find out who your local industry is made up of: the photo agencies, stock photo agencies, production companies, studios, equipment houses, and other vendors. Who are the prominent photographers in the genres in which you're interested, which agencies represent them, which production companies have they worked with, and where have they shot? The term "players" also extends to corporations or brands that contribute to the photography landscape as we know it—camera and equipment manufacturers, camera and equipment retailers, post-production services,

CHAPTER 1 | PAY YOUR DUES

editing services, professional photo management services, and photo organizations (more on those later), to name a handful. Familiarize yourself with the individuals, businesses, and various organizations that comprise the industry at large.

READ INDUSTRY NEWS

Keep a pulse on industry trends, new products and services, copyright news, industry innovators, and grants and awards by subscribing to photo industry news publications like Photo District News (PDN), Aperture, and Resource magazines. Blogs like PetaPixel.com, APhotoEditor.com, Photoshelter. com, and Fstoppers.com are also great sources of information and commentary that are written and moderated by industry peers. (See a full list of recommended publications, websites, and blogs under Resources, page 200).

Research

communities

JOIN A PHOTO ORGANIZATION

Professional photography organizations offer a wealth of resources and services to members. Most organizations charge a membership fee, dependent on experience, but it's well worth the information and support you'll receive. In the United States, the largest and most popular professional photography organizations are the American Society of Media Photographers (ASMP), American Photographic Artists (APA), and the Professional Photographers of America (PPA), but each country has its own set of professional photography organizations that are well worth reseraching yourself.

JOIN ONLINE PHOTO COMMUNITIES

Getting involved in online photo communities can be a great source of information and support. Not only do you have the opportunity to discuss photography with peers via online forums, you can upload your portfolio and receive expert critique from other photographers and industry leaders. Excellent communities exist on 1x.com, The Grid (which also features great webcasts), 500px.com, and Lightstalking.com—though there are countless others. Networking site LinkedIn also features many active discussion forums within professional groups; it's an good place where photo-industry professionals can network, debate, ask questions, and shoot ideas off one another.

**AMERICAN SOCIETY OF
MEDIA PHOTOGRAPHERS, INC.**

**150 NORTH SECOND STREET
PHILADELPHIA, PA 19106-1912**

**WWW.ASMP.ORG
215-451-2767**

Demetrius Fordham
Demetrius Fordham Studio

MEMBER NO: MEMBER SINCE: VALID THROUGH:

Associate

WORKSHOPS, SEMINARS, & EXPOS

Many photography organizations offer real-world workshops and seminars led by successful working photographers and industry leaders. Topics range from practical and skills-centered tutorials (e.g., improving digital workflow, how to shoot portraiture) to wider industry discussions (e.g., the copyright war, the future of digital photography). Events such as the annual PhotoPlus International Conference and Expo also offer a wide selection of lectures and panel discussions that bring together the entire industry. You'll also be exposed to a whole world of equipment vendors, camera and lens manufacturers and retailers, industry publications, and innovators—it pays to do your homework (see Research Key Players, page 18).

FIND A MENTOR

Whether you're a photo assistant or a photographer, it's beneficial to have a mentor—preferably someone whose career and work ethic you admire. Most likely, mentors come in the form of more illustrious photographers you assist or have assisted for, or successful colleagues who have been in the industry for many years. Outside the set, the best education you'll receive is from sitting down with a mentor and hearing the lessons they've learned over years. A mentor can also be a great source of contacts, business advice, and feedback regarding your own work.

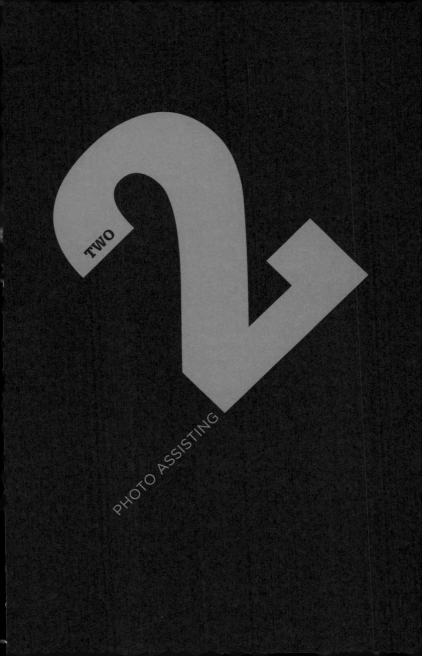

TWO

PHOTO ASSISTING

Volunteering or interning at an equipment-rental house or photography studio are great ways of familiarizing yourself with pro photo gear, and give you a front-row seat to real-life productions. But, once you are fairly comfortable with handling equipment and understand how a working set operates, you'll want to step out of the sidelines and into the action by becoming a photo assistant.

Author Note
Iconic photographers like Elliott Erwitt, Patrick Demarchelier, and Robert Frank started their careers as photo assistants. It's a serious and well-accepted path into the industry, and your own career.

As a photo assistant, you'll work closely alongside professional photographers, helping them scout locations, manage the set, set up lighting, and manage digital workflow, among so many other things. You'll learn things that a textbook or lecture never could have properly taught you—on-set jargon, the shoot anatomy, industry politics and the overall business of photography—all while rubbing shoulders with actual clients, producers, creative directors, assistants, and stylists. If you're lucky enough to assist a photographer you admire, you're watching an artist in operation, and this can be incredibly inspiring and fulfilling. Perhaps the most rewarding thing about assisting is that you're actually part of the action—and integral to the production's success.

It might sound like a lot of added pressure and responsibility—it is—but photo assisting is the best entryway into a photography career.

WHY ASSIST?

There are many other benefits that come with photo assisting, beyond it being a path to full-time professional photography:

"You'll get so much out of assisting if you have a humble attitude and are very open to learning. Obviously it's a good way to get paid, but you have to treat it as so much more than just that, because the most important thing you're getting out of it is the training, the exposure, and the understanding of the industry."

CAMERON SMITH
PHOTO ASSISTANT

EDUCATION
No photo-school professor, lecturer, or textbook could ever compare to shadowing and assisting a pro on the job. You won't get a more thorough photography education than working on set, from tackling seemingly mundane tasks like organizing equipment and setting up lights, to the more crucial ones, like helping the photographer achieve the desired shots.

NETWORKING
Besides photographers, you'll also get the opportunity to rub shoulders with a variety of other industry professionals: producers, clients, stylists, make-up artists, and models, among many others. But the most valuable kind of networking—at least during these early days—will be with fellow photo assistants. You'll learn that these social connections will pay off professionally, too, as photo-assistant friends can be a source of regular work for you and vice versa (see Getting Work, page 30).

CHAPTER 2 | PHOTO ASSISTING

Trajectory

CASH!

For many new and emerging photographers, photo assisting still remains their bread and butter. It's the best way to make a living while trying to secure regular shooting work and build your portfolio. The added bonus is that you're still learning while you're earning—think of it as getting paid to hone your technical skills and train with the pros until you're ready to run the show.

DIRECTION

At the very least, you'll acquire a clearer understanding of the photography business and how you want to be involved in it (if you still want to be involved in it at all!). You'll quickly discover the realities of the fast-paced and highly competitive photo industry: the bidding wars (for commercial photographers), the 4AM call times, the long days, and the difficult clients. For some, assisting only cements their desire to be a pro photographer; for others, it serves as an introduction to other industry professions like producing or even retouching. In any case, you'll likely achieve more clarity about your own career trajectory. Being a photographer isn't for everyone, and assisting is the best way to find out if it's for you.

TYPES OF PHOTO ASSISTANTS

There are several kinds of photo assistants:

THE FIRST ASSISTANT

The first assistant works closest to the photographer before and during the photo shoot and is essentially an extension of them. Prior to the shoot, the first assistant will assist with various logistical and technical pre-production tasks including scouting locations and securing second and third assets. During the shoot, the first assistant is responsible for lighting, camera settings, test shots, and overall set management, while constantly anticipating the photographer's needs. After the shoot, they will assist with post-production tasks like returning equipment and the processing and archiving of images.

Author Note
For a detailed breakdown of on-the-job tasks specific to each assistant, see On the Job, page 34.

SECOND & THIRD ASSISTANTS

The second and third assistants are generally managed by the first assistant and do most of the "grunt work." Physically laborious tasks like loading and unloading grip trucks, moving equipment, setting up and breaking down lights, holding reflectors, and setting up stands all fall under the second or third assistant's job description. This is usually where you'll start if you are new to the industry, and work your way up from here.

THE DIGITAL TECH

The digital tech is responsible for handling and protecting the job's most precious assets—the photographs. Throughout the shoot, they are responsible for managing and organizing image data, on-set comping, on-set retouching, color management, printing, and backing up. In post-production, they might be responsible for image processing and client-drive preparation (all depending on the particular photographer's preferences; sometimes the first assistant is tasked with this role).

GETTING WORK

Forget basically everything you've been taught about traditional employment: for assistants and photographers alike, there are no job applications to fill out or company websites advertising vacant positions. It's not as simple as listing your skills on your resume, sending it to a prospective employer, and then waiting for an interview. Getting work in this competitive and highly unconventional industry is not a straightforward process, but rather requires the multiple approaches outlined below.

RESEARCH

Thanks to the internet, tracking down the contact details of a photographer for whom you want to work is a fairly easy task—if a simple Google search won't pull up their website and contact information, then search for them on LinkedIn or Facebook. Before reaching out to them directly, it's wise to find out who their studio managers or first assistants are (typically the ones responsible for freelance-assistant hiring). If you live in the same city, chances are you'll have at least second- or third-degree connections, as local industries are often very small. Invite them out for a drink, or keep it strictly business and email them with your intentions. (Though take it from experience—everyone likes a free drink.)

LinkedIn

I know that just saying "go network" can be frustrating to hear, but it's a legitimate process that really builds up a momentum once you get the ball rolling. I would think long and hard before refusing anyone's favor or saying "no" to a gig, no matter how small— at least at the start. These small acts are the things that can cascade into a valuable group of contacts, each with their own resources.

NETWORKING

Make friends with other assistants. It might sound simple and commonsensical, but it's absolutely crucial. Having colleagues as friends will benefit you for the obvious social reasons, but in an industry so reliant on connections and recommendations, it will benefit you professionally, too. Most photographers rely on their first assistants to hire second and third assistants and even digital techs, so having a network of solid assisting buddies can help to ensure decent and regular work. It goes without saying that when you start to book your own photo-assisting gigs (or better yet, your own shooting gigs), you'll throw a bone their way, too.

Networking

COLD CALLING

Boldness pays off because so few people are willing to put their necks on the line and take big risks. Directly cold call the photographer with whom you'd like to work and tell them you want to assist them. Even if you don't land the job upon first contact, your proactiveness and go-getter attitude will have made an impression, and you'll stay in their mind for future jobs. Alternatively, call a production company and tell them you'd like to be placed on their assistant's list. After some vetting on their end, you'll be placed in a database and called on a needs basis. It sounds overly simple, but there is a lot of work that comes directly from production companies.

WORD OF MOUTH

The photo industry runs on word of mouth, so you must strive constantly to develop an excellent reputation (see Etiquette, page 53). In order to get recommended by the various photographers and producers with whom you work, have a consistently good attitude and work as if every job were an audition for the next one. It might very well be.

"Word of mouth is a wonderful thing in this industry. It is small and word gets around if you do a good job. Of course, if you have an attitude or mess up, people will remember that as well."

QUINTON JONES
DIGITAL TECH & RETOUCHER

ON THE JOB

Although there's nothing that can truly prepare you for being on set or in the field, the following will give you an idea of what you can expect before, during, and after an assisting job.

PRE-PRODUCTION—THE FIRST ASSISTANT
As a first assistant, you can expect to be responsible for at least the following pre-production tasks:

Logistics: Whether it's a big-budget commercial production or smaller, two-person shoots, you'll likely be involved in various conversations about logistics with the photographer, studio manager, and/or producer, depending on the size of the production. "Logistics" might include the renting of equipment, the hiring of second and third assistants, and even the coordination of pick-ups and transportation. For smaller productions, it's not uncommon for the photo assistant to pick up the photographer and other assistants and drive them to set, so have your driver's license ready.

Equipment: Generally, the photographer will send you an equipment list directly, but if you work with them regularly, you may be asked to put the list together yourself. The equipment list will outline all the cameras, lighting equipment, digital equipment, and expendable items needed for a particular photo shoot. Equipment is rented or purchased based on this list, to be picked

"I have seen more assistants fired or never hired again from being too mouthy. I know a number of competent, experienced techs that don't get my call to fill in because of the vulgar jokes they share to everyone or generally behaving like a know-it-all who can do what they want."

QUINTON JONES
DIGITAL TECH
& RETOUCHER

up personally by the first assistant (in some cases, second or third assistants) or delivered directly to set. In either case, the first assistant is responsible for checking that (a) all the equipment required in the order is present, and (b) all the equipment is in good condition and works perfectly prior to shooting. If you are picking up from the rental house or studio, you should manually test all equipment before leaving, and take photos immediately of any equipment that doesn't seem 100%. For smaller shoots with less equipment, this process is obviously less involved and the photographer might handle the pick-up of equipment themself, if any additional equipment is even needed.

"Study the photographer's website and get familiar with their work before the shoot. Know their shot list and schedule, understand the job's requirements, and know what you're there to do."

ELLEN ERWITT
OWNER/PRODUCER,
BIG SPLASH
PRODUCTIONS

Location scouting: A photographer will scout a location prior to most photo shoots outside of a studio (see Scout Your Location/s, page 114), and you will generally accompany them. It's important to keep an eye out for:

- **Power:** Are there enough power sources to run all the equipment, or will you need to rent a generator? How many generators might be required, and where will they be set up?

- **Lighting:** Is there enough natural light, or will you need to bring in artificial light? If it's an outdoor location, what is the best time of day to shoot in terms of sunlight?

- **Logistics:** Does the location have an elevator? If not, how many flights of stairs does the equipment need to be taken up? Does this require more manpower, or additional time to set up?

Naturally, the photographer should also look out for these issues, but they're often preoccupied with the aesthetics of the site—so take it upon yourself to do some basic technical and logistical problem solving, and discuss your concerns with them prior to the shoot.

CHAPTER 2 | PHOTO ASSISTING

PRE-PRODUCTION—
SECOND & THIRD ASSISTANTS

Second and third assistants aren't responsible for any specific pre-production tasks—you're usually hired for shoot day only—but the following will better prepare you for the job ahead:

Read the call sheet: Know exactly who is going to be on set, what their exact role is (for a detailed breakdown of roles, see Who's On Set, page 117), and know your own role. Have an idea of how the shoot day will be structured.

Read the equipment list: Familiarize yourself with the equipment that will be used on the day of the shoot. Know the purpose of each piece of equipment and how it should be set up before you arrive on set.

Ask questions: Not familiar with a specific piece of equipment? Logistical question? Call up the first assistant and ask. No question is stupid; being a second or third assistant is your time to learn the ropes.

CHAPTER 2 | PHOTO ASSISTING

PRE-PRODUCTION—THE DIGITAL TECH

Digital techs, like second and third assistants, are usually hired for shoot day only—and in some cases, certain post-production tasks—but the following will better prepare you for the job ahead:

Check digital equipment: Prior to shoot day, make sure the photographer or photo assistant didn't leave out any crucial digital equipment (including software such as up-to-date digital-capture software, Adobe Photoshop, etc.) in the equipment list. Don't just assume it's a given that you'll show up to set and all the necessary equipment will automatically be there. Always check beforehand, and don't be shy about asking for all the resources you require to do your job.

Do your homework: If it's the first time you're working with a photographer, reach out to digital techs with whom they've worked previously and ask about their digital-workflow preferences. Check with the photographer or first assistant whether you're expected to just perform basic "teching"—managing digital workflow, archiving, and backing up pictures—or anything more involved, like comping, retouching, and printing.

"More often than you would think, digital equipment is considered by many as just a computer. But if the first assistant forgot to put a camera cart or even the tether cable on the equipment list, it will be you that is blamed for it in the end. Any job that is on location or outside a studio, in particular, deserves double-checking. You can't do your job as effectively without at least a laptop stand on a tripod and some batteries for the computer."

QUINTON JONES
DIGITAL TECH & RETOUCHER

ON SET—THE FIRST ASSISTANT

As a first assistant, you are responsible for the following on-set tasks:

Set up: Your initial tasks for the day include helping the second and third assistants unpack the equipment truck, organizing equipment, setting up lights, building the cameras, rigs, assembling the camera cart, and any manual set up required prior the shoot.

Camera checks: Ensure that the aperture, shutter speed, and ISO are set to the photographer's specifications and that the camera has been set to capture Raw files.

Lighting: Ideally before the clients arrive, get crystal clear on the desired lighting. You should have already discussed this when putting together the equipment list, but it's better to overcommunicate than be unclear. Be clear on what lights are to be used for what shots, and prepare accordingly. Test the light by taking photographs of the second or third assistant, and make proper adjustments. If a lighting diagram is necessary to recreate identical lighting over a series of images, this falls under your job description, too.

CHAPTER 2 | PHOTO ASSISTING

"Attitude is just everything. Everyone starts from the bottom, so just be open minded and humble about it. Find the professional photographers you want to emulate, assist them, and learn from them. Along the way, you will work your ass off and make sacrifices that you never imagined, but if you stay positive, believe in yourself, and never give up on your dream, it will all pay off in the end."

DOUG MENUEZ
COMMERCIAL &
DOCUMENTARY
PHOTOGRAPHER

Set management: Even if a producer is on set, make sure your second and third assistants are on point. Even during lulls, they should be tidying up equipment or keeping busy—there's always something to do—and not texting, tweeting, or Facebooking (see Etiquette, page 53). You should also constantly anticipate the photographer's needs throughout the day. If they've been shooting uninterrupted for many hours or seem irritable or stressed, ask if they'd like some water or coffee, or a bite to eat. Do whatever you can to make the shoot run better and smoother—no task is too big or small in this role.

ON SET—SECOND & THIRD ASSISTANTS

As a second or third assistant, you are responsible for the following on-set tasks:

Set up: Your initial tasks for the day include unloading equipment from the van or truck and getting it to set, helping the first assistant organize the gear, and then preparing the set for production.

Power management: Whether you're in studio or on location, it's your job to run power to and from set from the power source or generator. Set up extension cords from the source to the ballasts, strobe packs, or other powered lighting equipment—anything that might need power.

Lighting: Throughout the shoot, you'll help the first assistant create the desired lighting; this involves taking light meter readings, and holding up lights, light modifiers, and reflectors as necessary.

Organization: Keep gear meticulously organized and easily accessible—you should know precisely where every piece of equipment is at any given moment. Have backup batteries, clamps, and gaffer tape ready at all times. It's also advisable to tidy up while you work.

Author Note
Being safe on set is also more than just preparation—it's keeping a sound state of mind as you're rapidly moving and setting up gear. It may seems smart to jump up on a table to quickly adjust something, but don't get swept up in the moment—think through what needs to be done and ask for help when you need it.

On-set safety: Safety is everyone's responsibility, but take it upon yourself to prevent equipment-related safety hazards. Make sure all lights are properly rigged and sandbagged, ensure there are clear walking paths, tape down all loose cords and cables with gaffer tape and have them coiled properly with Velcro ties when not in use, and double-check that all stands holding up backdrops or props are locked down properly.

ON SET—THE DIGITAL TECH
As a digital tech, you are responsible for the following on-set tasks:

Set up: The first thing you should do is set up your digital station: get laptops or towers situated and hook up calibrated external monitors. If required, set up tethered shooting, set up on-set monitors and/or viewing tablets for clients, even printer if work prints are needed.

Color balance: Take test photographs using a colorchecker card or 18% gray card to ensure correct color balance prior to shooting. Use an X-rite monitor color-calibrating system to ensure the color balance is accurate on-screen. Show the photographer your test images and ensure you're both on the same page about the desired look before shooting begins.

Digital workflow: While you've got the photographer's attention, get clear on digital workflow preferences: file names, capture folders, and digital backup.

Data management: You're responsible for handling the job's most valuable assets: what happens after image capture is all on you. You might also be tasked to perform Raw conversions, color-correction, and on-the-fly retouching.

Image monitoring: Watch out for focus, ensure exposure is consistent, and tag any outstanding images in real time so they're easily to pull up later and don't get lost in the shuffle. Basically, keep your eye on the actual quality and detail of the work that's being shot while you're archiving it.

POST-PRODUCTION

Post-production refers to "wrapping" the job (including returning of equipment), archiving and processing images after the shoot, and delivering the images to the client. As second and third assistants are generally hired for shoot day only, there usually aren't any post-production tasks specifically delegated to them. Digital techs also are not usually delegated post-production tasks—though they'll help prepare data for post-production, it's normally then handed off to the first assistant or photographer. In some cases, the digital tech might also be hired for their retouching services (it's quite common that digital techs are skilled at both tasks, as many are required to do on-the-fly retouching on set). But in most cases, it's the first assistant alone that handles post-production, namely the following tasks:

Equipment return: Equipment must be packed up and then returned to the studio or rental house from which it was taken.

Equipment cleaning: Cameras and lenses belonging to the photographer should be collected and cleaned after every shoot.

Wrapping the job: This involves archiving the job, usually at the photographer's studio, and uploading them to a central server, where the photographer's complete image archive is stored. You might also work with the client and photographer during the edit process, print work prints, collect retouching notes, and send the final images to the retoucher or retouching studio with said notes.

Post-shoot debrief: It's important to discuss any technical or communication-based problems that occurred at any point during the shoot with the photographer—especially if you work with that photographer frequently. Devise preventative measures to ensure these problems don't happen in future shoots.

Cables, like card readers, will usually be already present on set, but it's always useful to have back-ups. Basic cables like FireWire 400 and 800, faster cables like Thunderbolt (for Apple computers) and USB 3, and other connecting cables (such as a Mini Phono) for connecting remote triggers to strobe packs are good to have in your toolkit.

Though it's not required, it's advisable to have a basic assistant's kit with you on all jobs—even if you're a digital tech. Though you might examine the list below and wonder why a digital tech might need a Leatherman or set gloves, you'd be surprised at how often the need for these items arises. Always remember that it's a team effort, every step of the way, and it's better to be that person that saves the day than the person running around frantically on-set trying to track down random tools and items in vain. Stock your kit with the following items (the first four are the most important) and you'll always be in good shape:

A Leatherman or multitool: Though the idea of carrying around a Leatherman might seem archaic to some, the classic 21-tool "magic" pocketknife—complete with pliers, screwdrivers, wire cutters and strippers, and more—comes in extremely handy even on modern-day photo shoots. Whether it's tightening a loose stand, screwing a quick-release plate onto a camera (and off of it), cutting gels, fixing a light, or cutting sash cord, a Leatherman will still do the trick beautifully.

Set gloves: A good pair of lightweight, non-slip set gloves not only gives you a better grip on equipment, it also allows you to adjust a hot light without getting burned. They also come in handy

Author Note
Consider this a starting toolkit—as you observe the various sets and workflows of the photographers your assisting, you'll recognize certain specialized equipment that would be very smart to have on hand.

when handling dirty electrical cables, and will keep your hands warm and functioning when shooting on location in cold weather.

Gaffer (or gaff) tape: This incredibly strong, pressure-sensitive, ultra-adhesive, cotton-cloth tape can fix practically everything. It'll tape down cords, secure cables, flag a light, reinforce superclamps, hold cloth backgrounds in place for portrait sessions, attach props to shelves or the floor, temporarily "repair" equipment, color-code rentals on set, fix light-leak issues—the list is endless. In an ideal world, multiple rolls of gaffer tape would be already present on every set, but this isn't always the case, so it never hurts to throw a roll into your kit.

A Sharpie: You'll quickly find that there are a million uses for the humble Sharpie on set. A small handful include marking off things on set (often used in conjunction with gaffer tape), making technical notes (like the power setting on a strobe pack from one shot to the next), drawing up lighting diagrams, and writing names on water bottles and lunch orders.

A light meter, or sun-seeking apps: Despite what some may argue, light meters are still relevant, even in this digital age: they offer considerably more detail than the built-in meter inside a digital SLR, and can improve your pictures in certain scenarios. If you're photographing a model, for example, you'll be able to record the light on several parts of their body, add these figures together, divide to get an average, and then achieve the most accurate exposure.

Lens rag & cleaning solution. These are especially important on location, when elements and stray matter can find their way into your gear.

Allen key: Also known as a hex key, they're useful for fitting stands and tripods.

Box cutter: These are useful for cutting gels, reflector boards, and set paper.

Tape measure: If you're using a manual-focus lens, a tape measure will help you determine the distance between the camera and subject. They're also useful for determining the distance between the subject and lights when creating lighting diagrams and trying to replicate specific lighting scenarios.

Card reader: It's always good to have a back-up card reader in case one goes down (if you've ever owned a digital camera, you'll most likely have one on hand anyway), or if the tether cables malfunction.

ETIQUETTE

While the photo set is not your typical workplace, certain rules of etiquette still apply. If you're interested in getting hired again, heed the following:

Be punctual: Punctual in this industry means early. Allow time for traffic, delayed trains, missed buses, whatever. If it will take you half an hour to get to set, leave an hour before you need to be there. You don't want to arrive even a minute late; it's rude and unprofessional.

Check your ego at the door: Walk onto that set knowing that "assist" is the key word. You are the photo assistant, not the photographer (you'll have your time soon enough). In the meantime, learn how to respect someone else's shoot, follow instructions, and don't try to be the center of attention. Also, though you might know your stuff, never volunteer your opinion about a photographer's (or art director's, or stylist's) work without being asked first.

> "When it comes to the job itself, there's a saying: if you are on time, you are late. In other words, be at least fifteen minutes early. Particularly if it's your first job with a new production company. The producer is usually on set before the photographer, and will be on the lookout. Your alarm not going off is not an acceptable excuse. It is rare to get a second chance if you are late."
>
> **ELLEN ERWITT**
> OWNER/PRODUCER,
> BIG SPLASH
> PRODUCTIONS

Knowing

"You may have to interact with the subject on set, and it may well be a celebrity. As a rule, try not to talk about yourself, even if they ask; just keep focused on the task, and watch what the photographer is doing."

DOUG MENUEZ
COMMERCIAL & DOCUMENTARY PHOTOGRAPHER

> "Focus on the job at hand and be discreet. Being humble and having excellent manners goes a long way."
>
> **PETER "POBY" POBYJPICZ**
> COMMERCIAL PHOTOGRAPHER

Don't talk too much: It's fine to be friendly, but nobody likes a loud mouth or a storyteller. Do not, under any circumstances, flirt with talent on set—or anyone on set, for that matter. Speaking with fellow assistants for the purposes of the shoot and even networking is fine, but do so discreetly and in a way that does not disrupt production.

Turn off your phone: If possible, turn your phone off while on set, or at the very least, put it on silent. Don't text, email, Facebook, Tweet, or Instagram while you're working. If you must return an urgent call, do so quickly and discreetly during lunch break or a lull. For the duration of this job, your full attention should be on the production alone and not what's happening in the outside world.

Quickly

"Assume it's never okay to take set photos without the explicit permission from the photographer and producer. Do not post on Facebook, Instagram, Twitter, or other social-media outlets while on the job or afterward. Aside from the implicit non-disclosure nature of every job, no producer or client wants to see someone staring at their phone on set."

ELLEN ERWITT
OWNER/PRODUCER,
BIG SPLASH
PRODUCTIONS

Look professional: You may not have to wear a suit and tie, but you should still look presentable. This means avoid looking too trendy (can you really move around in those skinny jeans?) or too unkempt (there's a huge difference between casual and hobo). Statement shirts or shirts with any kind of political message can also stay in the closet. Try not to draw unnecessary attention to yourself: wear dark, simple clothes that are comfortable. When it comes to footwear, stick with sneakers or work boots—absolutely no Ugg boots, sandals, or flip flops, for the obvious safety reasons. Also: no chewing gum! It's just not a good look.

"I know some assistants who turn up to set looking like a homeless person— baggy, ripped jeans, dirty T-shirts, like they'd just rolled out of bed. Nobody would say anything out loud, but we were all thinking the same thing. It's a kind of disrespect, really. These assistants aren't hired again."

CAMERON SMITH
PHOTO ASSISTANT

FINANCES

Knowing how to handle your finances is especially crucial in the early days when you're just beginning to establish yourself—bad money habits can set the financial tone for the rest of your photography career. At this point, you don't need to hire a professional to help you; that will come later (see Hire a Business Accountant, page 168). But you do need to know the basics:

ASKING THE MONEY QUESTIONS

Though it might sound intimidating, it's crucial to ask the money questions right off the bat. After all, you're doing business and you need to know exactly what you'll be getting in return for your services. Before you accept any job, ask: What's the day rate? Is there OT (overtime after ten hours)? Is the job advertising or commercial? Are the travel days paid? It's not fun, but handling your business at the very beginning ensures that you're not wasting brain space thinking about money on the day of, and that everyone's on the same page, payment-wise.

KNOW YOUR RATES

You'll learn fast that no matter how much money a company, publication, or photographer has, they might still try to squeeze on rates—they're doing business, too, after all. But if you know your standard rates, you're less likely to get taken advantage of.

Author Note
Talking with fellow
assistants about
your rates is much
more accepted than
discussions of salary in
most other professions,
so don't be shy (don't
brag either—be smart
about it).

For U.S. photo assistants, editorial (magazine) rates should be $250 for a ten-hour day. It's common to hear $200 or even $150 from some publications—which was fine in the 80s—but if you think your time and services are valuable, fight for that $250.

For commercial and advertising work, $350 for a ten-hour day is acceptable, but first assistants that work regularly for the same photographer on commercial jobs can command day rates of $400 and upward. Digital tech rates, for both editorial and commercial work, start at around $500 for a ten-hour day. While this might seem like a lot in comparison to the assistant rates, the responsibility of singlehandedly managing the digital assets of a photo shoot is worth that money.

For editorial and commercial work, time-and-a-half after ten hours is the norm. Make sure you keep track of how many overtime ("OT") hours you've done so you can bill accurately and ensure you don't get short-changed.

For rate information on any other kinds of photo assisting (portrait, landscape, outdoors), or standard international photo assisting rates, contact your local photography organization.

Payment

BILLING & INVOICING

Unlike regular nine-to-five salaried employment, you won't get paid automatically after every assisting job—you'll need to bill for your services each time (it's good training for client billing later on in your career). You'll usually bill the photographer directly, as they will have hired your services, but clarify the exact billing details before the job even begins, so that you can shoot off the invoice right after the shoot. Some tips on invoicing:

Invoice directly after the job: Send in your invoice as soon as the job has been completed—the day after, or as soon as you can—while the job is still fresh on everyone's mind. Also ensure you submit any necessary tax forms (in the United States, it's the W9) to the photographer, in order to get paid faster. See a sample photo invoice at ilexinstant.com/resources/wtdtyips. Also submit any work-related receipts, if any expenses came out of pocket.

Find out your payment date: Always ask the photographer or appropriate billing contact when you can expect to be paid. The standard is usually within 30 days. The most important thing is to determine in what time frame you'll be paid, so that you know when to follow up.

Insider Tip: Keep all your receipts! Scanned copies of any production-related expense receipts—food, transportation, excess baggage fees during travel—should accompany every invoice. Keep copies for tax time, too, either in a folder or using digital receipt-keeping programs like Expensify, Shoeboxed, or NeatReceipts.

Streamline your system: Scrupulously track all your outgoing invoices; monitor what money you've received and what payments are still outstanding. Billing programs like Blinkbid make this easier by keeping track of all of the above and even sending you email reminders when payments are due. Keeping everything organized will also allow you to keep an eye on your steady revenue stream (or lack thereof)—crucial for freelancers like us.

Author Note
Even though it can feel awkward, never let your gratitude for the work overshadow the need to follow up on a payment—it's a regular part of business, and the client is often expecting it anyway.

FOLLOWING UP

Even if you've followed all the steps up to this point, the sad truth is that there's no guarantee you'll get paid when you want, even if you're getting the rate you want. You shouldn't wait more than 30 days to get paid—if you've hit the three-week mark and still haven't gotten your check, follow up with a quick email.

In reality, payment can sometimes take over 30 days. In these cases, use your own discretion. If it's a photographer you've worked with before and who is doing their best to pay you, then you might let it slide with weekly friendly reminders until you get a check. This typically works, and should usually get you paid within a couple of weeks outside the initial 30-day mark. Should it take any longer than that, sign up for Square. It's a smartphone app/device that allows you to accept credit-card payments, which will give the photographer, production company, or agency the ability to pay you promptly, while buying them time (ideally with the money they receive from their client, by the time their bill is due— although that's not really your problem). Any longer than 60 days and you can consider small-claims court, or reach out to your local photography organization for advice or action on your behalf.

SAVING & BUDGETING

Constantly winging your finances is a recipe for disaster. Keep an eye on your money, and monitor your daily, weekly, and monthly finances. Track your general expenses: non-business related costs like housing, gas, utility and phone bills, cable subscription, gym memberships, and scheduled automatic payments. Knowing your monthly overhead can highlight what costs might be excessive or unnecessary, and help you allocate your funds better. The easiest way is to break it down via percentage—e.g., set aside 10% for savings, 25% for rent, 10% for food, 5% for health, 10% for transportation, and so on. Having your funds properly allocated will ensure that your bases are covered, at all times.

Budgeting

TRANSITIONING INTO SHOOTING

Full-time

If being a career photo assistant is something that fulfills you, there's certainly nothing wrong with that! But if you—like most assistants—are using it as a stepping stone for a career in professional photography, here are some tips for making the gradual transition.

SAVE YOUR MONEY
The importance of saving and budgeting in general was discussed in Finances on page 63, but having a nest egg—however small—is essential in making the transition into full-time photography. Living from one assisting paycheck to another makes it difficult to take time out to build your portfolio and market yourself as a photographer. You should ideally come to the point where you're able to turn down assisting work in favor of shooting gigs that might not pay much but will help elevate your career. This is almost impossible if you're constantly scraping by and in need of cash, so squirrel away everything you can, while you can.

Think of photo assisting as a way to invest into your dream as a photographer. Be smart with the money you make during this time because when you're finally starting to let go of assisting and taking on photography full-time it can be rough financially. Your days of working per month might decrease significantly, and those initial rates might not be high enough to support yourself at the beginning. So save as much as you can while you're still assisting, and later, until you can afford to go at it full-time, keep a balance between assisting and shooting

PETER "POBY" POBYJPICZ
COMMERCIAL PHOTOGRAPHER

en I was starting out, things were
y different. A photographer hired y
a full-time assistant, and then you
ntually start getting jobs via referra
n the photographer—they'd even
d off jobs to you that they didn't
nt. Once you got yourself a few
ges, a small portfolio, you'd cut
cord and then start on your own.
vadays, the break is less distinct.
v, there might be a period where
shoot and assist, or do something
on the side like retouch, tech,
rip. It's more of a patchwork affair
nding shooting and assisting
k, simultaneously."

ERT WRIGHT
RIAL & PORTRAIT PHOTOGRAPHER

BUILD YOUR PORTFOLIO

You must first have work in order to get work, so you'll most likely begin shooting for free in between assisting jobs. This is where networking pays off: If you've done it properly, you should have other professionals around you—assistants, stylists, make-up artists, and studio managers— who are open to helping and supporting you during these early days (see Assets & Resources, page 76). Shoot as much as you can in the beginning. Perfect your shooting skills, develop and refine a style, pick a genre (see Find a Specialty, page 80), and build a portfolio around that. Don't worry if it seems incomplete at the beginning—it will continue to grow and change as you land more work and mature professionally.

DEVELOP A BRAND

Figure out early what exactly is your distinct style, your "thing," that special flavor in your images that makes it uniquely you. It's beyond a specialty or niche, though these certainly help to inform your brand. It's more of a way of distinguishing who you are and why you are different from the next fashion photographer, or the next family portrait photographer. (It also makes it easier for you to narrow your images down into a tight, powerful portfolio). Like your portfolio, your brand might change and adapt as you progress in your career—but it's something you should constantly be thinking about in these early stages. Having a strong, recognizable brand makes it easier for potential clients to decide to hire you, because they already know exactly what they can expect.

MARKET YOURSELF

Get online! Create a website and put your portfolio on it. Start a blog; get active on Facebook, Twitter, and especially Instagram (where many emerging photographers have been discovered). Subscribe to an international industry database like Agency Access, and send out emails and print promos to the editors, producers or ad agencies with which you'd like to work. All the rules outlined in Marketing and Advertising, page 150, apply here 100%.

APPROACH CLIENTS

This is a highly competitive industry and you'll need to fight tooth and nail for jobs. All the rules for getting work as a photo assistant also apply to photography jobs: be bold, cold call, and set up meetings (leverage the assisting contacts you've already made and get them to make introductions). These meet-and-greets might not land you a job straight away, but you'll come to mind when they need a photographer in the future.

Author Note
Only a few years ago, it was very common to think you were too cool and your art was too authentic to ever possibly resort to marketing yourself through social-media platforms. People got over it. It's standard operating procedure now, and foolish to not take advantage of this valuable outlet.

Three

STARTING OUT

Improve

So you've paid your dues as an intern, volunteer, or photo assistant, you've done your homework on the industry, and you're ready to jump headfirst into the life of a professional working photographer. While that's great and you can certainly go right ahead looking for work (see Getting Work, Chapter 4), it's a good idea to spend some time simply "setting yourself up" before the madness ensues.

Ensuring that you have the right basic equipment, arming yourself with useful assets and resources, and figuring out a photography specialty before you start building your portfolio and chasing jobs will give you a better chance of success and helps to eliminate wasted time, money and effort early on. The problem with most new and emerging photographers is insecurity, a lack of focus, and being unsure of "where to start," which can lead to bad decision-making, poor allocation of time, and, all too often, the purchase of expensive, unnecessary camera equipment as compensation for a lack of experience. There might be a lot of pressure to be a successful working photographer straight away, but try to ignore or at least temper it. Your primary focus in these early days should be on improving and perfecting your shooting technique and discovering exactly what kind of photographer you are.

WHAT YOU'LL NEED

You'll begin to collect the accoutrements of a working photographer as you progress in your career—namely, high-end pro photo equipment—but starting out, you don't need very much in your arsenal. It's easy to be enticed by expensive cameras and fancy lenses but in the beginning, your main investment should be the time and effort you put into perfecting your photography.

That said, as you begin to pick up more and more shooting jobs, a handful of essentials are required. It's necessary to have basic photo equipment, like a solid starter camera, a bare-bones toolkit, and image-capturing/processing software, plus a few resources that will make your life considerably easier in these early stages.

THE STARTER KIT

If you have the money to shell out on fancy pro photo equipment from the outset, then by all means do. But if you don't, it doesn't make a difference—the camera don't maketh the man (or woman). When you're starting out, you don't need a whole lot in terms of essential equipment; the following will get you well on your way.

Essential

The temptation early on for many people is to accumulate as much gear as possible, even going into debt because of it, and that is a very dangerous thing. The debt, obviously, is a bad idea—but also the flood of possibilities early on might confuse your learning curve. The old saying, 'one camera, one lens' is a good rule for those starting out."

ROBERT WRIGHT
EDITORIAL & PORTRAIT PHOTOGRAPHER

"Don't get carried away—all you truly need in the beginning is a good camera to practice and shoot with, and a lens or two. Remember, you can always rent out anything extra that you need for a job."

PETER "POBY"
POBYJPICZ
COMMERCIAL &
DOCUMENTARY
PHOTOGRAPHER

The camera: Forget the expensive, medium-format Hasselblad—any full-frame DSLR will make a solid starter camera. Canon and Nikon make great quality basic models that are reasonably priced and have easy-to-rent lenses and accessories. Other camera manufacturers like Olympus and Leica are great, but aren't as ubiquitous on the shelves of photography rental houses internationally. Both Canon and Nikon also offer Professional Services memberships, which feature lifetime camera repairs and servicing, and valuable resources for working photographers.

The lens: You'll need a high-quality professional lens, preferably with at least a 24–70mm zoom range (35mm equivalent). You don't need a fancy Zeiss lens to begin with, either; Tamron offers great, inexpensive lenses that will do the job.

Basic tools: For now, basic light-shaping or light-modifying tools will be sufficient. This can be something as simple as a 3-in-1 reflector or a basic strobe kit. A Leatherman or any kind of multi-tool, cube taps, gaffer tape, and sun-seeker apps on your cellphone are always good to have on hand, too. If you're primarily shooting landscapes or nature photography, you'll also need to purchase a tripod. Manfrotto make solid, mid-range tripods that should more than suffice.

Image-capturing software: A laptop loaded with industry-standard image-capturing and processing software like Adobe Photoshop (on the most basic level) or Capture One Pro (what professionals use), is essential. If you don't know how to use these programs, you can access free pro tutorials on Lynda.com. It's also a good idea to have a 500GB (or greater) bus-powered portable hard drive on hand to back up all your images.

ASSETS & RESOURCES

The following assets and resources are optional, but highly recommended during these early days of shooting.

Photographer's insurance: Having photographer's insurance to protect your own personal equipment, insure all the equipment you rent, and guard yourself against liability should anything happen on your set is essential, even if you're just starting out—especially if you're just starting out. In fact, most equipment rental houses require it, or will otherwise hold the replacement value of all rented equipment up front—this could mean thousands of dollars held on your credit card—until items are returned in perfect condition. Photographer's insurance is offered at a discount through a number of professional organization memberships, or through specialized insurance providers.

A vendor base: Your vendor "Rolodex" will continue to grow the more you work, but at the beginning you should at least set up accounts with an equipment rental house and a photo studio for your basic shooting needs (if you can find a studio that rents out equipment, even better). Once you have your vendors, stick with them through the years, as they are more likely to give favors and discounts to loyal customers. In the U.S., ResourceMagazine.com has a good

"The best money that an emerging photographer can spend is certainly on comprehensive insurance coverage. We require that any person or production that comes through the door carry their own insurance for their protection. Photo and film sets are dangerous places: we see equipment like C-stands not properly set up, or grip equipment at risk of coming undone. It's not only for equipment either—it's also to cover liabilities in case someone gets injured on set. Having photo insurance is a standard professional practice and is expected of everyone."

PETER CLARK
OWNER, NEW YORK
CITY'S ATTIC STUDIOS

CHAPTER 3 | STARTING OUT

and growing vendor directory; internationally, ProductionParadise.com has a similarly good directory. Your national professional photography organization is also a great resource for local vendor recommendations.

Manpower: As you begin to build up your portfolio, you're going to need as much help as you can get. You must first have work in order to get work, so you'll most likely begin shooting for free and will require some good old favor-based manpower. Fellow photo assistants to whom you can "pay back" in voluntary services are ideal production assistants and digital techs in these earlier shoots. Many emerging stylists and make-up artists will also be willing to work in exchange for professional photographs of their work (ModelMayhem.com acts as an international directory of stylists and MUAs).

"It pays to have a go-to studio. Not only because you know what equipment they have and the benefits and limitations of that studio, but also because it's a place you can go to when you have a budget— and when you have no budget. Having a relationship with the managers or owners of a studio helps when you just want to shoot a test, or build your portfolio, or you just aren't that flush with cash."

PETER CLARK
OWNER, NEW YORK
CITY'S ATTIC STUDIOS

"Be creative! If you can't pay for setting up a shoot, find local models who are looking to get portfolio images and head shots who will trade—it's a sharing economy. You can also use family and friends as subjects, and as extra hands on set."

ELLEN ERWITT
OWNER/PRODUCER, BIG SPLASH PRODUCTIONS

FIND A SPECIALTY

While it's nice, in theory, to think of yourself as a one-stop shop for every kind of client's photography needs, it's hard to succeed as a "generalist" photographer. From a client's perspective, it's better for you to be a master at shooting one thing than average at shooting everything and anything.

Author Note
Nailing down your specialty can be tricky. Sometimes you can be exceptional at a particular skill, even though that may not be a part of your absolute favorite genre (e.g., a passionate street shooter who's amazing at building lighting setups). If you find that you're getting consistently positive feedback on something outside you're normal area of interest, pursue it, and see where it leads.

That said, you'll need to determine exactly what kind of photography you want to do. If it's not already clear to you, you can find your specialty through assisting on different kinds of productions (see Photo Assisting, Chapter 2), research, or merely looking at the kind of photographs you're drawn to and the photographers that you most admire. Or you can simply get out there and explore what exactly you like shooting (see Tips for Starting Out, page 84–89).

Most people will find that they already have an inherent preference for a certain type of photographic genre. You certainly don't need to limit yourself strictly to one kind of photography—it's not so cut-and-dried, and you'll likely overlap throughout your career—but having a basic specialty will help you build your brand and helps clients understand what you're all about and what they can expect from you. The main specialties are:

Fashion: Fashion photography is devoted to the display of clothing, shoes, jewelry, and accessories, usually on models. The role of a fashion photographer is to conceptualize and capture fashion products in interesting and exciting ways. Work will typically come from magazines, catalogs, advertising agencies, and fashion houses. Notable fashion photographers include Helmut Newton, Nick Knight, Peter Lindberg, and Richard Avedon.

Portrait: In portrait photography, the person, or groups of people, are the main focus, as opposed to their clothing, environment, or backdrop. Generally, a photographer will try to capture the individual's expression, personality, or mood. The focus of the photograph is often the face, although the entire body may be included. Work will typically come from magazines and publications, advertising agencies, and corporations. Notable portrait photographers include Annie Leibovitz, Mary-Ellen Mark, Irving Penn, and Cindy Sherman.

Product: Product photography encompasses everything from food and beverage products to still lifes of accessories and clothing items—quite a broad subject. Work will typically come from catalogs, magazines and publications, advertising agencies, and fashion brands.

Author Note
A relatively new and rising genre in which a lot of photographers are finding success is e-commerce. Photographers who specialize in e-commerce create product and catalog photography meant primarily for web uses—often for the sale of products or apparel online. Work will most often come from fashion brands and advertising agencies.

Outdoor & Landscape: Photographers who specialize in shooting outdoors aim to capture nature and the elements. Work will typically come from travel magazines, outdoor apparel brands, and advertising agencies. Some talented outdoor photographers have partnered or been sponsored by corporations such as RedBull, GoPro, and Nikon. Notable outdoor photographers include Ansel Adams, Arte Wolfe, and Corey Rich.

Event: Event photography includes but is not limited to weddings, corporate events, parties, festivals, and concerts. Event photographers may also be commissioned by publications to cover specific featured events. Clients typically include magazines, newspapers, corporations, festivals, and private clients.

Photojournalism: Photojournalism is rather different from other genres of photography, in that the images are used to tell a news story and are generally not manipulated. As it is journalism, there are strict editorial standards for honest and objective photography. Work will typically be limited to news publications and occasionally not-for-profit organizations. Notable photojournalists include Sebastião Salgado, Elliott Erwitt, and Henri Cartier-Bresson (the father of the genre).

TIPS FOR STARTING OUT

It's completely natural to be overwhelmed at the beginning of this journey—on top of trying to navigate a completely new industry, there's the struggle of balancing assisting with shooting, building your portfolio, and getting work, among other pressures. But don't throw in the towel yet! Photography can be a deeply exciting and fulfilling career once you've overcome these initial hurdles. The following tips might not necessarily make these tumultuous early days any less challenging, but they can help you get started on the right foot.

PRACTICE

Utilize this time to practice your technique and perfect your craft. Use your camera every day, even when you haven't been commissioned to shoot anything. You don't have to head out in pursuit of an award-winning shot seven days a week, and you don't even have to organize any formal photo shoots, necessarily. The important thing is to just get out there and take pictures, and allow yourself to be inspired and stimulated by whatever hits you. Play with composition and light (light is everything). Try doing themes: portraits one week, landscapes another week, indoors vs. outdoors—anything goes. Try everything—it's the only way to discover what kind of photographer you really want to be. Experiment with multiple settings to learn what effects you like (when you're looking at your photos on a computer, you can check the EXIF data to recall the settings you used). Some of this may well feel like you're back in photo school, but there's absolutely nothing remedial about exercising your creative muscles. It may seem cheesy, but tasking yourself with these activities really does pay off in the long run. The only way to become a master at photography is by practicing, constantly, and it's something you should continue doing throughout your career.

ASK FOR FEEDBACK

As I mentioned in Chapter 1 (See Join Online Photo Communities, page 20) there are a number of excellent forums online where you can upload your images and have them critiqued by other photographers and industry leaders. 1x.com, The Grid on Kelbyone.com (it features a great monthly webcast dedicated to blind photo critiques), 500px.com, and Lightstalking.com are good options, though there are countless others. If you're reluctant to have your work examined by strangers (which is fair—some people visit these critiquing sites with nothing but malice in their hearts), then ask for feedback from industry peers or a mentor (see Find a Mentor, page 22). At some point—preferably when you've developed a more robust portfolio—you should attend a formal portfolio review (see Your Portfolio, page 92) but for the meantime, online and peer feedback is a good start. Pay attention to recurring comments and work to incorporate solutions into your work.

CREATE AN INSPIRATION BOARD

Yes, it sounds corny. But collecting images of work that you admire and keeping them in plain sight (on a pinboard, in a scrapbook, or even on your computer desktop) can be incredibly useful for boosting your own creativity. It's important to note here that you're not trying to copy other artists' work—rather, you're cherry-picking certain elements from different photographs that you'd like to emulate or incorporate into your own word. It will also help you better understand the style of photography you're drawn to, particularly if there's a distinct theme across most of your chosen photographs. Plus, as a photographer you should be constantly surrounded by art that inspires you.

THINK ABOUT BRANDING

You don't need to obsess about branding at the very beginning (I'll cover that later in Marketing & Advertising, page 150), but it's never to early to start thinking about what makes your photography unique. Why you are different from the next commercial photographer, or the next family-portrait photographer, or the next fashion-editorial photographer? What's your trademark, that "thing" in all your work that makes it distinctly yours? Defining your brand shouldn't be rushed or forced; just keep the idea of it in mind as you create work and it will usually begin to reveal itself naturally.

SET GOALS

While you should develop large, long-term goals for your photography business (see The Business of Photography, Chapter 6), setting small, short-term goals are just as significant, especially in the beginning. Even one or two weekly goals (e.g., some in-studio test shoots, and approaching a dream client) will help you inch toward success, and will give you the sense of accomplishment you need to persist when things don't go your away.

GET ON SOCIAL MEDIA

The importance of social media is covered extensively in Getting Work, Chapter 4 and Photography in the Digital Age, Chapter 7, but it's also necessary to note here that every aspiring photographer today must have a strong social-media presence. The reality is that if you don't exist online, you don't exist at all, so create professional accounts for Facebook, Twitter, Instagram, and LinkedIn. It's the easiest way to get your name out there and connect with industry professionals like photo editors, creative directors, and producers (they're all on social-networking sites). The more active you are in uploading photos and engaging with followers, the more exposure you and your work will get. Think of social media as free marketing—it is.

"The junior editor on your assisting gig will age at the same rate you age, and when you are shooting, he or she will be editing. So don't give anyone attitude. It's a long career and a small industry. All of your peers and juniors will be around a lot longer than you imagine—so treat people nicely."

ROBERT WRIGHT
EDITORIAL & PORTRAIT
PHOTOGRAPHER

BE NICE TO EVERYONE

Yes, everyone. Treat third assistants or grips with the same respect you'd give creative directors or ad executives. Despite what the call sheet hierarchy might be, nobody is better or more important than anybody else, and each person is there to help get the job done. Being a diva or having an ego does not impress anyone.

HAVE FUN

Everything else aside, keep taking photographs primarily because you love doing it and because the chief reward is the process itself. All the pressures of succeeding, landing work, and being recognized will come soon enough—they might have already!—but in for as long as you can, hang onto that sheer love of photography for dear life.

Respect

4
FOUR

GETTING WORK

You've paid your dues, your shooting skills are on point, you've figured out your specialty, and you're armed with the essentials needed to kick off your photography career. But how do you actually go about getting hired?

Photography is an unconventional industry in that there's no job application to fill out or company website advertising vacant positions. Traditional job interviews don't really exist, and the only résumé most photographers will ever need is their portfolio. But in some ways, it's similar to conventional employment in that connections and "who you know" can lead directly to job opportunities. In fact, in this industry, most employment is based purely on connections, recommendations, and word of mouth.

That's not to say that it's completely impossible to generate work organically in this industry— it's just harder. Aspiring photographers can still book jobs through sheer, unrelenting persistence. Clients are just people too, and they can be convinced (if not eventually worn down) into throwing you a bone. And at the end of the day, that one job is all you need. If you do it well, it will most certainly lead to others.

Author Note

I wanted to shoot an editorial for a particular magazine for a long time, so I'd constantly reach out to their creative director with my updated portfolio, ideas for photo shoots, or just to say hi. Anything to make a connection. This all happened for about a year before I got an email from the creative director, out of the blue, asking if I'd be interested in shooting an editorial for them. Whether they were blown away by my talent or I just wore them down with my incessant (but professional!) contact, I got that job. The rest, as they say, is history.

YOUR
PORTFOLIO

Showcasing

Before you go out seeking work, you'll need a portfolio. Your portfolio is a carefully edited selection of your work, showcasing the kind of photography in which you specialize, and your unique brand of photography (See Create Your Brand, page 150). Some experts insist that a portfolio should show off your career's best work and the breadth of your shooting skills, while others argue you should have several portfolios, each tailored to a specific client that you're approaching. The truth is, there is no right way to put a portfolio together—so long as it appears seamless, reflects who you are as a photographer, and eventually gets you hired.

It's important to note that portfolios change and adapt over time, just as you will artistically. Don't be discouraged if your portfolio starting out isn't as robust as you'd like—perhaps you're still figuring out your specialty and your brand, and this is okay. The important thing is to work on continually improving your photography and progressively curating it into a strong, tight, powerful portfolio, with the critique of experts.

PORTFOLIO TYPES
Digital: Having your portfolio readily accessible online, preferably in website form, is essential in this digital age. (See Create a Killer Website, page 174). You should also put together a PDF portfolio to send potential clients directly.

Hard copy: There is still value in having a physical, hard-copy portfolio that you can bring to portfolio reviews, potential clients, and advertising agencies. Electronic images and the internet are convenient, but they're less beautiful and inorganic to some. There is still something to be said about touching and holding a beautiful book of images. That said, your portfolio doesn't need to be fancy, leather-bound, or even expensive—a clean, neat, barebones portfolio that lets your work speak for itself is more than sufficient.

TIPS FOR A SOLID PORTFOLIO

HAVE A THEME

Your entire portfolio should flow seamlessly and demonstrate a clear, unified style or theme. You're essentially trying to sell your brand and communicate what's unique about your photography. You might be especially proud or fond of a particular photo—but unless it's consistent with your primary body of work, leave it out. Which leads to the next point.

BE RUTHLESS

Your portfolio should contain no more than 20 images—preferably no more than 15—so do a hard and tight edit. Photo buyers, clients, and production companies are extremely busy, so every photo should wow them and be worthy of their time. If you're in doubt about a photo, it probably doesn't belong there.

CONSIDER YOUR AUDIENCE

If you're trying to score a fashion photography gig, it might not be a good idea for half of the portfolio to be reportage or nature landscapes. It's better to curate different photographs into separate portfolios tailored for specific clients.

CHAPTER 4 | GETTING WORK

"Here's a secret to the portfolio-reviewing process: I'm looking for reasons to not hire you—images that I think are awful, bad models, poor styling, and so forth. You've got to edit as tight as you possibly can. Don't throw a couple of mediocre images in to increase your range. As soon as I hit a few duds my mind turns to the dressing down I will get from my editor if images like this end up on his desk."

ROB HAGGART
FORMER PHOTO
EDITOR & FOUNDER,
APHOTOEDITOR.COM

This is not uncommon; rather, it's highly recommended—if you have the time, patience, and resources.

START STRONG, END STRONG

It goes without saying that the first image should be your strongest—you are "announcing" yourself. That said, don't put your least strong image at the very back of your book. Leave potential clients with a similarly strong image so they'll walk away having been blown away.

GET AN EXPERT OPINION

Once you have amassed a larger body of work, experts can help show you where your images may fall short, or how to better edit your portfolio to attract your desired client. International photo festivals like the Palm Springs Photo Festival and the Hong Kong International Photo Festival give you the opportunity to connect with photo editors, agents, galleries, reps, and book publishers (see a full list of international photo festivals in the Resources section, page 200).

Opinion

NETWORKING

Networking is one of the most cost-effective yet powerful marketing and advertising strategies that exist for photographers (See Marketing & Advertising, page 150). The old adage that "it's who you know" rings true in most industries, but especially here. There are no shooting jobs advertised in the newspaper or on employment websites; hiring happens via recommendation. That's not to say that raw talent and persistence don't play a huge part—they do—but in the highly competitive world of photography, having connections will give you that leg up.

MAKE INDUSTRY FRIENDS

In the photo industry, friendships have benefits that extend far beyond the realm of socialization. Though photographers don't generally go about recommending other photographer friends for jobs they're vying for, they may recommend you for shoots they don't want or can't commit to due to scheduling conflicts or other factors. It also pays to stay friendly with clients, creative directors, photo editors, and producers with whom you've worked in the past. Don't hound them for regular quality time, but meaningful connections via email, or even just the occasional coffee can keep you fresh on their mind in case they or any of their connections require any services in the future. You've probably heard the saying "people do business with people"— it couldn't be more true with photography.

"It helps to have connections, but at the end of the day, you still need to be very good to land jobs. Having the right contacts won't ever trump talent."

PETER "POBY"
POBYJPICZ
COMMERCIAL
PHOTOGRAPHER

"Networking is
insanely important
in every industry, but
in photography it's
even more so, because
the opportunities
are just so few and
far between. People
hire the people they
trust and connect
with, so take the
time to build genuine,
lasting relationships
with people in
the industry."

DOUG MENUEZ
COMMERCIAL &
DOCUMENTARY
PHOTOGRAPHER

EVENTS, MEETUPS, & REVIEWS

If it's about "who you know," then get to
know people! Find out what kind of photographer
meetups and events are happening in your area
through your local photography organization—
chances are, they're sponsoring many of them—
and just go. The popular site Meetup.com also
advertises many photography-related meetups
where you can get together with other working
photographers in your area who are likewise
looking to network. Attend photo festivals and
expos. Go to real-world seminars and workshops
(see Get an Industry Education, page 18) to
learn and to rub shoulders with other industry
professionals. These classes are excellent
opportunities to build long-term relationships
with fellow photographers and teachers. Portfolio
reviews are also a great way to get face-to-face
with the editors, photo directors, gallery owners,
and curators with whom you want to work,
while simultaneously getting feedback on your
portfolio. Just remember to follow up afterward!

GET ON LINKEDIN

Being active on all social media is important
(see Get Social Media Savvy, page 181–187), but
LinkedIn can be especially useful for networking
with other photographers and industry pros.
One of the benefits of LinkedIn for photographers
is the ability to join relevant LinkedIn groups—
e.g., on commercial, fashion, or wedding

Author Note
I once met an assistant photo editor randomly on a DPReview.com forum. He used his real name as his handle (I followed his publication closely, so I knew exactly who he was) and we chatted at length about the Canon 5D Mark III (the topic of the forum). Later, I shot him a private message introducing myself as a photographer and asking for his email address so that I could send him my portfolio. He obliged, and we kept in contact. About ten months later, he emailed me out of the blue asking if I'd be interested in doing a last-minute portrait for his publication—the photographer they'd commissioned had fallen ill, and he remembered my work. Some call it luck, I call it networking paying off!

photography—and participate in discussions with other group members. You're probably not likely to get a job directly through LinkedIn, but, with over 277 million users at the time of writing, it's a serious way to "meet" people in the industry, and that can translate to real-world connections.

JOIN FORUMS

Being a member of a professional LinkedIn group gives you access to great online forums on topics and issues pertaining to that group, but there are countless open forums aimed at bringing photographers together for networking and discussion. ThePhotoForum.com, DPReview.com, and DGrin.com are popular online forums where photographers and enthusiasts alike come together to discuss gear and techniques. There are specific sections dedicated to professionals, with threads covering everything from the business of photography to professional workflow tips. Many photography news sites, blogs, and even photo organizations (like the Professional Photographers of America) also offer useful online discussion forums for readers and members—just look for the "Forum" or "Discussion" tab on their websites. Online critique forums like 1x.com, 500px.com, and Lightstalking.com allow you to meet other professionals while simultaneously getting peer feedback. You'll be surprised at how many professional connections start online.

HAVE A BUSINESS CARD

Have you ever bought a book simply because you loved the cover? Your business card is kind of like that: It's the first impression people have of you as a photographer, so make it a good one. Your business card should ideally reflect your branding, but when you're just starting out and don't have a wealth of resources at your disposal, all you really need is a great-looking card with your name, website link, email address, phone number, and (if appropriate) one of your best photographs. If you can't afford a graphic designer, you can design them yourself online—OvernightPrints.com, PremiumCards.net, and Moo.com are all great, and ship internationally. Always remember: Every time you hand out a business card, ask for one in return.

THE ART OF FOLLOWING UP

Following up is the best way to make your networking connections actually work for you, as opposed to just sitting around and waiting for that connection to reach out. If you do it right, it will give you a greater chance of a landing job.

There are many ways of following up, but email has always been the classic method. Always send a follow-up email within 48 hours of the initial meeting—it can even be a quick note saying, "It was great meeting you!" or "Thanks for your time!" If it's a potential client you for whom you

Insider Tip
Don't forget to follow up with clients with whom you've already worked! Send them new work, updated portfolios, or merely check in and let them know you'd love to work with them again. That way, you'll remain fresh in their minds the next time they need services.

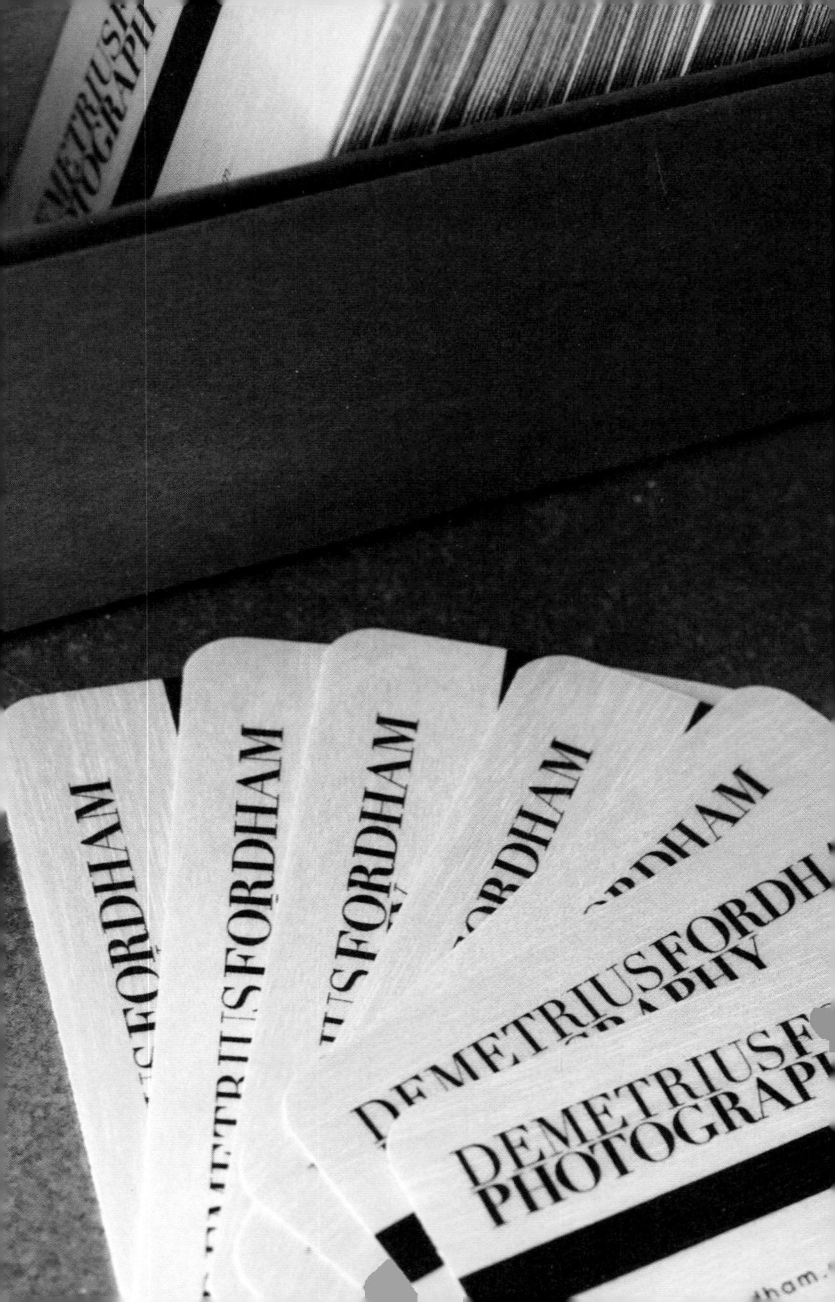
FORDHAM

Contact

want to work, check in regularly—once a month is just right—and try to be creative about it. Find out something about the contact that might pique their attention, like a link to an interesting article or an idea for a photo shoot. If you get a response, suggest casually meeting for a drink after work, or even offer to drop by their office with coffee and donuts (speaking from experience, this works). Once they've decided they like you, you're in.

If you've met a professional contact through much more casual circumstances—through friends, for example—it's acceptable to add them on Facebook, Twitter, or Instagram in lieu of an email. Actively use these avenues to remain in contact, even if it's just sharing an interesting article on their wall or tagging them in an interesting tweet or quote. If there are any upcoming industry functions you think could be worth attending, send over an online invite and suggest you check it out together. You don't always need to be pushing business, either—you can keep it casual and fun. Suggest you grab lunch or meet for happy hour. The real key here is to keep on the radar of contacts you've already painstakingly made via your networking efforts.

THINK OUTSIDE THE BOX

Besides networking, marketing and advertising are the main ways photographers attract clients and get hired (see Marketing & Advertising, page 150). But in this competitive digital age, it pays to think outside the box and be bold.

SHOOT PASSION PROJECTS

Be different. Break away from shooting what you think might get you paid photo jobs and just shoot what excites and inspires you, especially in the beginning when you're still trying to figure out your specialty (see Find a Specialty, page 80). If it doesn't fit into any traditional "box" or genre, that's fine—being interesting, innovative, and fearless pays off.

Photographer Phil Toledano was intrigued by individuals' "hidden characters," and hoped to capture them by photographing their expressions while playing video games. He was later commissioned by Nokia to shoot a commercial campaign inspired by his Gamers series. Similarly, self-taught photographer Brandon Stanton was inspired to take portraits of the people he encountered every day on the streets of New York City. These portraits were turned into a successful photo blog, which turned into a photography book that topped *The New York Times* Best Seller list in 2013. Stanton was also approached by fashion label DKNY with an offer to buy his pictures (which he refused).

Passion

"We are in a golden age of photography. It's never been easier to have pictures published, and you can quickly discover if an audience, beyond your relatives, exists for your pictures. So get your work out where it can be seen, and hustle as hard as you can."

ROB HAGGART
FORMER PHOTO EDITOR & FOUNDER,
APHOTOEDITOR.COM

"It is possible for a new or emerging photographer to be hired by reaching out cold to a photo editor at a magazine they want to work for. It can take several years to get your foot in the door, but you've got to start somewhere. It can't just be a cold call, though: portfolio viewing, direct mail, seeing your work in a magazine, a recommendation from a colleague, something on a blog online—these are also excellent points of contact that help with a hiring decision."

ROB HAGGART
FORMER PHOTO
EDITOR & FOUNDER,
APHOTOEDITOR.COM

GO TO THE SOURCE

Many photographers shy away from going straight to the source for jobs—particularly to big clients—because of beliefs that they're "not good enough," won't be taken seriously, or that a common friend or recommendation is required to make the connection. Sure, that helps, but if you don't have a direct connection, then just make one. You have nothing to lose!

Want to work with a certain brand? Find out which agencies handle that brand's commercial campaigns and reach out. Want to shoot for a magazine? Sign up for Agency Access or Adbase, find out the appropriate editorial contact, and reach out. If you can't find them on a database or can't afford to sign up, a sneaky trick is to look for the names of the photo editor and assistant photo editor in the hard copy of the magazine you want to work for. You'll find them in the masthead, just a few pages past the table of contents. If there's no phone number listed next to their name, call up the magazine's advertising department (for which there will always be a contact number). Tell advertising that you dialed the wrong extension and ask to be transferred to editorial. Once you're transferred to the editorial switchboard, ask to speak to the specific editor you'd like to reach (if it's a smaller magazine, advertising might just transfer you directly). Unorthodox, sure—but it works like a charm.

BE SEEN

The more exposure your work gets, the greater your chance of getting hired. You can no longer just rely on traditional marketing and advertising methods, either, though they can still be highly effective (see Marketing and Advertising, page 150). New and emerging photographers are under pressure to find new avenues of promoting and showcasing work. Look into having your photographs featured at local pop-up galleries, or put on a group show at a warehouse or events space with your peers. Boutique hotels in larger cities will usually have an artists-in-residence program showcasing local talent; many cafes and bistros also display and sell the work of local artists. Do your research and find places where you can put your work in the face of potential clients—you'll be surprised at the number of nontraditional options available.

SELF-PUBLISH

Thanks to the ever-increasing accessibility and affordability of high-quality printing and print-on-demand services, more photographers are now self-publishing their own photo books and seeing enormous career success. In 2010, emerging photographer Matt Eich won numerous awards for his self-published book, *Carry Me Ohio* (he was offered a solo show at the Houston Center for Photography shortly afterward), while Martin Adolfsson's *Suburbia Gone Wild* was

"My first big break was getting a photography internship at *The Washington Post*. In the end, what made the difference was that I flew to Washington and delivered my application, by hand, to the photo editor himself. I was starving at the time, living hand to mouth, so it was big deal for me. I ended up beating a thousand kids out for that job because I wanted it more. Talent takes you to the starting line; effort puts you in the race. Insane dedication gets you to the front of the pack."

DOUG MENUEZ
COMMERCIAL & DOCUMENTARY PHOTOGRAPHER

Author Note
Once you've got a product out there (anything from a blog post to a published book), it's essential that you follow through with the publicity. Creation is only the beginning; next you've got to make sure to get it in front of as many people as you can, and also to respond and interact with those people (particularly in an online context—there's nothing worse than seeing a big list of unanswered comments to the author of a post).

featured by numerous international news outlets, including *CNN*, *The Atlantic Cities*, and *Slate*. Those are just two success stories; self-publishing has become so popular that the bulk of submissions to photo book competitions are now from self-published photographers. It's not just books, either—with so much competition in the fashion editorial realm, many photographers are creating their own online magazines that showcase their work and the work of their peers. Think outside the box—in this digital age, why should you wait to be offered a book deal, or to have a published magazine editorial? Publish your own book, and create your own tear sheets. Create work to get more work.

GET A PHOTO AGENT

Though not impossible, it's unlikely that you'll land a photo agent at the very beginning of your career. It happens in rare occasions, but generally, agents prefer that a photographer has a stable of existing clients and regular work before representing them. That said, there are many agencies out there looking for photographers across all genres and levels of experience. So whether early or later on in your career, it can be worth seeking out a photo agent who will partner with you to define your brand, edit your work, protect your interests, and help you land more jobs. Here are some tips for finding an agent:

RESEARCH

If there are certain photographers you admire, find out what agency represents them. See if your work might align with their stable of artists or perhaps add something different or interesting to the mix. Have an idea of why you'd be a good fit for that agency. You might also look for an agent that works with your specific genre—say, outdoors and adventure photography—or within your geographical area. If you're an emerging photographer, it's a good idea to target smaller or mid-sized agencies to begin with.

Partner

> "Every month, you need to reach out to the editors or creatives that might be interested in your work. That might mean a call, a subtle campaign using direct mail, whatever. My rule of thumb is that it takes about one year of reaching out to one person to get a job from that person. First, aim to get a face-to-face meeting. Then, a few months later, go back with brand-new work, and blow them away. Then keep following up. Be persistent and never give up. Eventually, the right project will pop up and you'll land that job."

DOUG MENUEZ
COMMERCIAL &
DOCUMENTARY
PHOTOGRAPHER

EMAIL SUBMISSIONS

Send the agency a specially-curated PDF portfolio, a link to your website, and a very brief introduction to yourself. Photo agents are incredibly busy people who receive countless submissions per day, so keep it no longer than a paragraph. Let your personality shine through, and explain why your work would be a good fit for the agency.

SNAIL-MAIL SUBMISSIONS

Unfortunately, agents receive so many mailed submissions that only the especially unusual or interesting ones stand out. If you're hell-bent on sending a print submission via traditional mail, it's worth getting creative with it for the sole purpose of having it be seen by the agent. Pro tip: handwritten notes never hurt.

FOLLOW UP

Follow up about a week after submission with an email or a brief phone call. Be polite, remind the agent who you are and about your submission, and reiterate why your work would be a good fit. Don't be pushy, but do be persistent. Continue to stay in touch like you would with a potential client, until they have made an official decision about representing you. If an agent continues to entertain your follow-up emails or calls, this is a good sign—continue checking in around once a month and sending new work you create it.

5

> "The truth is, only around 10% of my time is spent actually taking pictures—the rest is writing proposals, pitch meetings, research, production, finance. Hard, tough work, every day. But man, that 10% sure is sweet. Glamorous? Someone else can judge. Regardless, taking pictures is the most fulfilling and satisfying thing I can imagine doing, so all the tough slogging is well worth it."

DOUG MENUEZ
COMMERCIAL &
DOCUMENTARY
PHOTOGRAPHER

In the real world of photography, being on the job doesn't involve simply picking up a camera and shooting it. If you started out as a photo assistant, you'll know that there is extensive planning and preparation involved before the shoot even begins. I'm talking hours of "desk work"—researching clients, finding locations, sketching, and storyboarding—long before you're out on the field. The shoot itself requires a great deal of mental preparation; you'll need to multitask, be highly organized, have a structure for the day, keep track of time, communicate effectively, handle stressors, and troubleshoot quickly. You may have to travel, and it will not be glamorous. Work-related travel involves weeks of dealing with documents, gear, and endless red tape. It's stressful, it's challenging, it's high pressure—and if you do it right, it can also be the best job in the world.

Welcome to the life of a working photographer.

Pressure

PRE-PRODUCTION

"From the ad agency's point of view, it's important for the photographer be fully involved in pre-production, especially location scouting. Even though the final decision is usually the agency's and/or client's, they will look to you for your opinion, so be prepared with your list of suggestions and selects. The creative team will be looking to you for your professional opinions from a photography standpoint."

ELLEN ERWITT
OWNER/PRODUCER,
BIG SPLASH
PRODUCTIONS

It's not just shooting prowess: the success of any shoot is dependent on how well you prepare for it. Some of it won't be up to you; for larger commercial and editorial shoots, most pre-production decisions like choosing models, locations, and even the overall creative direction of the shoot will fall on the clients and/or producers—but in any case, you need to be on top of the aspects you can control and do your homework. When there's a job to be done and money on the line, there is no such thing as over-preparation.

SCOUT YOUR LOCATION(S)

On smaller-budget shoots, you'll choose and scout locations solo. For larger commercial and editorial shoots, the clients and producers are generally responsible for deciding shoot locations, but it's important to get involved in the process. Get familiar with the client's requirements and offer your own input from your own experience or research. Clients can often miss interesting, photogenic locations simply because they aren't looking at it with a photographer's eye.

Once the final location has been "cleared"—the availability has been confirmed, fees have been discussed, and the necessary permits have been obtained—you should do a final scout prior to the shoot (particularly important for outdoor locations). Take note of the sun, direction of light, and time of day, and shoot test photographs to gain a better understanding of how the available light will look on camera. Get a sense of the site's surrounding geography—the adjacent buildings, the nature, the neighborhood—and think about it in regards to composition and details. Take note of where the equipment trucks and generators will be and how close to the site they are parked. (Location scouting for studios is generally more straightforward.) In any case, discuss any concerns you might have with your producer or the location manager prior to the shoot.

CREATE A SHOT LIST & STUDY IT

You can't possibly control everything on a shoot—when you're in it, the energy, people, and momentum come together and it will often take on a life of its own—but you can still create guidelines to help you achieve your desired outcome. You can do this by putting together a reference board or, better yet, building out a shot list prior to shoot day. It's as simple as getting out a notepad or sketchbook and drawing the key shots you want to achieve that day, and in what order (it's similar to storyboarding for a film). It will give you an idea of what your finished shoot will look like even before you arrive on set, as opposed to simply "winging it." Plus, planning out the rundown of shots won't just help you better bring the images to life, it will keep you more organized, sane, and less stressed during

the day. Note: Some clients may already provide
you with a shot list that includes the images they
require for the advertising campaign or editorial
that you're shooting. In either case, it's important
to know that once you've achieved your key shots
it's fine to go off-script and have some fun. Some
of your best shots can be the ones you take in the
moment, without reference.

WHO'S ON SET?

If you're an events photographer, portrait photographer, or photojournalist, you generally don't have to worry about a production crew—due to the nature of the job, you'll be running in small, one- to three-man teams. But if you're a commercial or editorial photographer, you'll be working on set in a much larger team, and must be informed accordingly. Who is your first assistant, second and third assistant (if any), digital tech, and PA? Who are the producers, clients, stylists, make-up artists, models? Study the call sheet and learn names and roles. It's not just good manners, it ensures you know who is accountable for what tasks and makes asking for things much easier when you're in the thick of the shoot. A quick rundown of roles:

Producer: The producer essentially handles the production of the shoot from its early stages to its execution. A producer (or producers) are necessary for larger or big-budget commercial or editorial productions, and will handle all the fine details, including flight bookings, location permits, job cost estimates, catering, and call sheets. During the shoot, the producer is behind the scenes "running the show," usually with the help of a production assistant, or PA.

Together

Client: In commercial photography, the client is a sweeping term for the people or company hiring you for your photographic services. This could include an advertising agency handling a commercial campaign, with all its marketing executives, art directors, art producers, and creative directors, a combination of which are generally present on set. In editorial photography, the client is generally the creative department of the magazine or publication that commissioned your services. In any case, the client will review and select images and have the final say.

Art department: Depending on the needs of the production, this generally consists of the prop stylists, set builders, and/or set designers. Together, the art department is responsible for physically building the set, dressing it to its desired aesthetic, and bringing it to life.

Photo assistant: The role of the photo assistant is to support the photographer during the shoot; to basically act as an extension of the photographer—anticipating their needs, preparing cameras, lenses, and equipment, and overseeing everything from lighting to image capture and workflow. See a detailed breakdown of photo assistant types and responsibilities on pages 30–31.

Author Note

Don't for one minute think that you're more important than any of the rest of the crew—there's no quicker way to look unprofessional. Everyone is there to do a job, and all of these jobs are important.

Wardrobe, make-up, & stylists: Fairly self-explanatory—these people are on set to create the desired look on the talent.

Talent: The models or actors featured in the shoot.

Gaffer, electrician: On bigger-budget commercial shoots, there is usually additional tech support on hand. The gaffer would handle heavy-duty lighting and rigging, while the electrician might be responsible for handling specialty power requirements.

Craft services: Self-explanatory—usually a catering service. One of the producer's PAs will generally ensure that everyone is fed, hydrated and caffeinated throughout the duration of the shoot.

Author Note
If you know you're
going to be shooting
in a variety of
conditions, it also
pays to set up your
camera's custom
shooting modes in
advance. These let
you save a plethora
of settings (autofocus
modes, exposure
settings, picture styles,
etc.) under a single
setting, which you
can switch between
very quickly. It's much
faster than diving into
the menus every time
you change subjects
or scenery.

CHECK ALL YOUR EQUIPMENT

If you're flying solo, double-checking all your
equipment is already a given. But even if you're
working with an assistant who you've tasked to
prep the shoot, at the end of the day, it's still your
job to get the shot. So take thirty minutes the night
before every shoot to:

- Check your batteries and ensure that they
  are fully charged.
- Check your sensors are clean, and if not,
  clean them.
- Clean your lenses.
- Make sure all memory cards are formatted
  (not just erased; formatting improves the
  overall performance of a card).
- Test all equipment before it leaves the
  rental house, or ensure your assistant does.
  This includes the most basic of equipment
  like tripods: make sure their locks lock,
  legs don't slip, and heads don't wobble.
- Ensure your camera settings—aperture,
  shutter speed, ISO—are on point.

Prepare

ON SET

Taking great photographs is one thing, but maintaining Zen, working with others, communicating your needs, and managing stress levels while on a busy, crowded set is another thing entirely. As a general rule, successful photographers aren't just good at taking pictures, they're also good at managing and navigating their set—or any working environment—and are easy to work with.

ORGANIZATION

Things can get crazy fast on larger sets, so get all your ducks in a row as soon as you arrive. Your photo assistants might be responsible for organizing the equipment, but it's your job to be mentally organized during shoot day.

Have a structure: Having a structure for the day and a clear idea of the photographs you're going to shoot (see Create a Shot List & Study It, page 115) helps a lot.

Structure

organize

Keep track of time: It helps to have a strong sense of timing throughout the day by studying the call sheet and being conscious of how much time you have to nail each shot. You shouldn't let time restraints trump creativity, but definitely be aware of what you should accomplish in each "block" of time, and stick to it as best you can— you're here to get a job done, after all. If you need more time, communicate this to your producers as early as you can.

Have a Zen zone: Have your digital tech set up shop in a quiet place, so you're able to review images in peace. Controlling when your clients see your photos will help you keep your sanity; you don't want them looking over your shoulder and making comments (and criticisms) constantly. Some photographers don't mind the real-time feedback, but many photographers find it breaks their concentration and prefer some control over what images the client sees—and doesn't see. It's often better to invite clients in for feedback after your own initial edit.

Set up your camera cart: Like instruments laid out on a doctor's surgical table, your tools should be set up on your camera cart in equally organized fashion. Lay out your lenses, cameras, and extra batteries in a way that is most efficient and accessible to you. You don't want to have to dig for a different lens mid-shoot.

"If you have questions on the final work or amount of images needed or anything regarding a client's expectations, don't be embarrassed to ask. You're here to do a job. Communicate! Ensure that there are no misunderstandings."

PETER "POBY"
POBYJPICZ
COMMERCIAL
PHOTOGRAPHER

INTERPERSONAL SKILLS

Photography is a business, so it's important to pay attention to customer service. Be personable and courteous to everyone, including the assistants and PAs—they are all there to make the production run smoothly and help you get the job done. Make people feel good about what they're doing and give praise where it's due. Learning how to communicate effectively on set is also crucial; it is essentially a machine comprised of many different parts working in tandem. If you're in doubt as to whether or not an essential task has been taken care of, don't assume it has—ask. Overcommunication is always better than wasting people's time.

TROUBLESHOOTING

No matter how prepared you are, at some point, problems will arise on set; it's simply the nature of production. Equipment can get lost or stolen, people will get sick, talent can fall through last minute—the list of potential issues, big or small,

Don't

Keep Calm & Carry On

The most important thing here is to just keep doing your job, even if you've messed up. It's all to easy easy to feel incompetent, embarrassed, and shut down, but these things happen and the show must go on regardless. Pick up the camera and get the job done.

is endless. Learning how to manage these stressors and quickly troubleshoot them is key. These tips might seem commonsensical, but when you're overwhelmed, common sense is the first thing to go out the window.

Don't panic: Panic isn't just counterproductive; it's infectious! Instead of panicking, find out the source of the problem. If it's something you can fix, then communicate how much time you'll need and what you'll require, and then troubleshoot. If it's out of your control, find the person best suited to help. It's usually that simple.

Focus on the bigger picture: Most mistakes are rectifiable—merely a hiccup in production. Don't give it more weight than it deserves. However, if the mistake severely impacts the final outcome of the shoot—i.e., the photos were not backed up and therefore lost entirely—take a moment to breathe, calculate your losses, and then focus on damage control.

TRAVEL

"The travel part of it might look luxurious, but when I'm working, every cell of my body thinks photography. I trained and prepared for six weeks to get ready for an assignment in Fiji. I sat on a wooden plank on a boat in the burning sun, holding up a 300mm *f*/2.8 for many straight hours, to shoot surfing action shots. Nothing fancy about that. But my fun is when I capture a killer image. It's wonderful and I'm grateful I can make a living doing it."

PETER "POBY" POBYJPICZ
COMMERCIAL PHOTOGRAPHER

What's even better than getting paid to take pictures? Getting paid to travel and take pictures! Though that sounds glamorous, it's often also twice the work. Think about it: you're essentially packing up thousands of dollars worth of professional photography equipment and schlepping it across the world, with assistants and an entire production team in tow. You'll deal with visas and work permits, equipment documentation and insurance, airline luggage limits and excess travel expenses. On bigger-budget commercial and editorial shoots, you'll have a producer to help with logistics, but if you're working with a small budget or your own personal projects, you'll need to tackle it solo. And that's on top of all the regular pressures of shooting, working on a set, and meeting client's expectations, all while trying to shake off the jetlag! Don't be mistaken—there's still nothing quite like seeing the world while getting paid to take pictures, and with some careful preparation, the experience can be seamless and enjoyable.

Sometimes it's a smart
move to get a seat at
the rear of the plane,
so that you can board
before others and thus
make sure you have
enough space to stow
your bags overhead.
You don't want to get
to the door and be told
you'll need to gate
check your bag full
of gear—the attendant
probably won't care
about how valuable
it is.

BEFORE YOU FLY

Flying to another country for a photo shoot is
a little more involved than flying for vacation—
you'll have about three times as much luggage
and three times as much paperwork (if you're
lucky). Trip preparation begins weeks, sometimes
months, in advance of your scheduled flight, due
to the sheer amount of documentation required
for yourself and your equipment. These are the
basics you'll need to get together before heading
to the airport:

Passports, visas, & ID: Ensure that have your
personal travel documents in order: namely, an
unexpired passport (some countries require six
months' validity before entering, so renew your
passport as necessary) and the requisite work
visas. A producer will generally assist with visas,
but it is still your responsibility to ensure all your
documents are in order to avoid delays. If you
travel frequently to and from the United States
for work, consider applying for the Global
Entry program, which will save you time and
paperwork, and offers expedited-entry benefits
to many other countries. You should also always
carry a valid driver's license, as you'll need it
for identification purposes and for international
car rentals.

Carnets: If you're traveling outside the country with multiple cases of high-value photo or video equipment, it's a good idea to obtain a carnet document (essentially a temporary "merchandise passport" for your equipment) to ensure you clear customs more easily and freely. These can be applied for online or at a carnet office, though in most cases the producer or studio manager will handle this process, and all you'll need to do is provide the serial numbers off each piece of equipment. Obtaining a carnet can be a tedious process, but traveling with it makes hauling equipment from country to country significantly less dramatic.

Credit cards: In a perfect world, production or job-related costs should never come out of pocket. But in reality, you'll need to put up your own cash for cabs, excess baggage, some meals, or to cover incidentals at a hotel. That said, carrying at least one internationally accepted credit card is necessary (Visa or MasterCard aren't likely to let you down). Once the job wraps, you're entitled to get all these excess travel-related expenses reimbursed, including international roaming charges on your cellphone, so keep all of your receipts and records to ensure you can justify all the expenses you're claiming. (See Billing & Invoicing, page 60.)

Author Note
Before you head to the
airport, load up on all
your properly packed
gear and take a walk
around the block. It's
the quickest way to see
if you can handle it all,
and you'd be surprised
how much more willing
you'll be to shed some
weight when you're
back home.

PACKING

The photo assistant is usually tasked with
packing the equipment and traveling with the
bulk of it, but if you're flying solo, you'll need
to pack everything yourself. Some tips:

- Check that you've packed all the small-but-
  necessary items: cables, batteries, chargers,
  travel adaptors, and memory cards. There's
  nothing worse than discovering you have
  dead batteries and no charger in a location
  with limited professional photo resources.
- Ensure all cameras are disassembled (do not
  have a lens attached to your camera) and
  individually wrapped.
- Use sufficient padding for fragile items like
  the camera body, lenses, and filters.
- Secure your equipment in sturdy, travel-ready
  camera bags or cases before checking them in.
  Tenba makes excellent cases with weatherproof
  material, thick padding, and integrated storage
  for camera, video, and digital equipment.
- Carry on all cameras if possible. This way if
  everything gets lost in transit or stolen, you
  are still able to take pictures.
- Pack properly for yourself, but travel light.
  Try to fit a week's worth of clothing into one
  bag. Ensure you bring one nice, collared shirt—
  you'll most likely be asked to dine with clients
  at some point.

Back Up Everything
Backing up images should already be standard practice for your photo assistants or digital techs, but due to the high risk of digital media getting lost in transit, you have to get obsessive about protecting your files when traveling. Ask your photo assistant or digital tech to give you the hard drive of images taken on the job while carrying a duplicate hard drive of images. It's also a good idea to have your assistant or digital tech FedEx one back-up hard drive of images to the studio's address before leaving the location.

TRAVEL SURVIVAL TIPS

Travel to a foreign country will always have its own inherent risks, but with so much on the line during work-related trips, there's an added pressure to mitigate these variables. The following smart, simple survival tactics will help keep you out of trouble when working in an unfamiliar destination.

Get a fixer: Having a local expert on the ground at your destination can not only be invaluable to the production itself (they can scout locations prior to the shoot, organize film permits, recommend local talent and crews if needed, and hire extra equipment), they can also assist with seemingly minor but crucial logistical tasks like transport to and from the airport, hotels, and locations. Most importantly, they know the territory, speak the language, and can use their specialist local and cultural knowledge to swiftly handle bureaucracy and other inevitable obstacles and road bumps.

Protect your gear: If you're going out to do some exploring with a personal camera in tow, protect it from theft—being a fairly small object that's highly valuable, it's an easy target. An effective method is to make your expensive camera look as old and undesirable as possible. Cover up logos and brands with duct tape, and carry it in a weathered old camera bag.

Author Note
I was traveling to the Congo for a photo shoot and landed at the Kinshasa International Airport late in the evening. I wasn't worried about entering the country since I had all the necessary documents in place—a valid passport, work visa, and the required vaccination certificate. So I was shocked when customs refused to clear me! From what I could understand, they had doubts about the vaccination certificate I had, and wanted to give me their own vaccine at an inflated cost—or send me back home. Thankfully, there was a fixer waiting for me at the airport that I was able to call upon. He spoke French, cleared up the situation in ten minutes, and saved me from what was potentially a very hairy situation.

Stay healthy: Long workdays coupled with jet lag and a fast-paced, high-pressure environment aren't so great for your general well-being. It also doesn't help that you'll often have dinner after the shoot with the crew and sometimes clients, and may be tempted (or obligated) to stay out for a drink or hit the town. Though it's nice to socialize and explore a new city, you need to have enough sense to know and respect your limits. Get back to your hotel room at a decent hour and try to get at least six hours of sleep—seriously. Even on "free" days, fight against jet lag and try your best to wake up at local time. Drink lots of bottled water. It also doesn't hurt to have a dose of Cipro on hand, just in case.

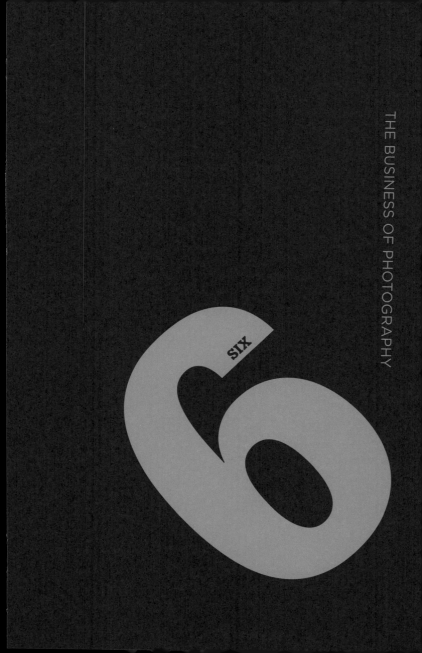

SIX

6

DEMETRIUS FORDHAM
PHOTOGRAPHY

demetriusfordham.com
info@demetriusfordham.com
646.641.6973

> "This business requires you to have a clear direction and know exactly where you want to go in order to succeed. This is not a nine-to-five job that you can simply forget about on weekends—you need to live and breathe photography if you want to make a living from it. Take your business seriously, and others will take you seriously."
>
> **PETER "POBY" POBYJPICZ**
> COMMERCIAL PHOTOGRAPHER

You're most likely pursuing photography because you're a creative, not a businessperson. I get it—you just want to get out there and take photographs! But if you've been reading this book chronologically, you'll know already that photography is a serious business; you're offering a service to a client, and if you want to make a successful living from it, you must treat it like one. Finding a niche, developing people and management skills, and knowing how to write an effective business plan is just as important as understanding lighting or knowing how to frame a shot. What separates successful photographers from amateurs and hobbyists is business acumen and a strong sense of professionalism.

Goals

WRITE A BUSINESS PLAN

The long-term success of most businesses hinges on good planning, and a photography business is no exception. Every emerging photographer should create a business plan that clearly outlines their goals and determines a course of action for achieving them. It doesn't need to be long or even particularly detailed or complex—in the beginning, it will be largely for self-reference than for securing a business loan, so a simple one- or two-page document is fine. But it should still have a clear mission statement, your revenue goals, and a business strategy. Remember, this isn't a hobby—it's your livelihood. You are in the business of taking pictures, and just "winging it" will only set you up for failure.

"It's critically important that photographers learn how to write a business plan. The thing that holds back a lot of potential photographers is not having a plan, they go from gig to gig and can get stuck. They don't have an understanding of the business side—the thing we all hate—and as a result, never have enough cash to do the shoots they want, or the portfolio and marketing that they need to establish themselves. It's necessary to write a business plan that clearly states what your dream is, and how you see that happening over however many years. The idea is to build a stable foundation that will let you fly free as an artist."

DOUG MENUEZ
COMMERCIAL & DOCUMENTARY PHOTOGRAPHER

Joel Anderson Photography is a New York-based portrait photography business committed to capturing the raw, natural beauty of each individual. I specialize in striking yet simple, clean portraits shot in natural light, offering a softness and authenticity to my editorial, commercial, and select corporate clients, in contrast to the highly stylized portraits of many competitors. I am driven by a passion for finding and capturing the essence and uniqueness of each subject, and beyond my services, I aim to find a personal connection with every client.

WRITE A MISSION STATEMENT

Summing up your photography business's mission will help you clarify your purpose and fundamental objectives, so that you can figure out the steps you need to take to succeed. In a few sentences, your mission statement should encapsulate the core purpose of your business, your goals, and underlying philosophies. There is no "right way" to write a mission statement—the important thing is that it inspires and reminds you of what you're doing, why you're doing it, and what you're aiming for. The following questions can help you formulate your mission statement:

Who is your target audience? What is their income level? What are their buying habits? What are their needs and pain points?

Why should clients choose you? What makes your brand of photography unique, interesting, or superior? How do you differ from competitors in the same genre? Don't be vague—write down what makes your services extraordinary, and what makes you stand out from the rest.

What exactly is your business? What specific services do you aim to provide? What's your specialty, your niche? What is your brand? (See Create Your Brand, page 150.)

Why are you in business? What do you aim for? What drives you—passion, a cause, creating beauty? Why did you pursue photography, and specifically this kind of photography?

What are your principles? What do you in? What are your values? What do you stand for? What's the "why" behind your mission?

What extra can you offer clients? There are literally millions of other photography businesses out there. How can you go above and beyond just being a photographer? What will keep clients coming back? Is your client's life just a little bit better because of your services, and if so, how? If not, how can you make it so?

TAKE STOCK OF YOUR FINANCES

We'll get into the nuts and bolts of managing your finances later in this chapter (see Finances, page 160), but for the purpose of the business plan you'll just need a very basic understanding of where you are financially, and where you want to go. This means identifying how much money you've made with your services (total sales), how much you spend for the business (cost of sales) and how much profit you're actually taking home at the end of the day (net profit). Knowledge is power! Having a grasp on your financial state allows you to plan and manage your business better, and then establish some revenue goals. Here's a simplified way of taking stock of your finances for your first business plan.

Monthly total sales: This is a record of how much money you're making with your photography services per month on average. In the beginning—unless you're already working quite regularly—it can be hard to get an accurate representation of your average total sales per month, as some months you might not book any jobs at all. But the beauty of a business plan is that you can use rough estimates initially, and then recalculate and refine these figures once your career really starts taking off. Don't get discouraged if this figure is quite low—you need to know where you are in order to figure out where you're going.

Calculate

Monthly cost of sales: This is a record of how much money you're actually spending for each shoot. Here, I'm talking variable, shoot-specific costs like one-time studio rentals, hiring photo assistants and digital techs, or editing fees. These are different to fixed business expenses, which will be explained later.

Monthly gross profit: Take your total sales number and subtract your cost of sales. This is how much money you are actually making from your photography jobs per month—but don't get too excited. This is not the money you'll necessarily go home with.

Monthly fixed business expenses: This is the average cost per month of your combined general expenses—anything that you need to keep your business running. These include website hosting fees, membership fees, and marketing. You should also add what you want to pay yourself each month—a number that should be conservative in the beginning but should still cover all your own basic expenses.

Monthly net profit: Take your gross profit number and subtract general expenses. This is how much actual profit you've made in your business. Don't be discouraged if this is in the negatives—it can take at least a year to see positive net profits.

The most important thing at the beginning of your photography career is that you're fully aware of your financial standing, so that you're able to set yourself some revenue goals and outline strategies for achieving those goals. See Marketing & Advertising (page 150), Budgeting (page 167) and Multiple Income Streams (page 169).

DEVELOP A BUSINESS STRATEGY

A business strategy outlines the means by which a photographer will achieve the desired objectives of their business plan—in other words, your proposed "path to success." Naturally, each photographer's path will look completely different—there is o one effective strategy that can be applied across the board. Your own strategy will be dependent on your individual strengths and weaknesses, target market, competitors, and your own definition of what it means to be a successful photographer. The following exercises will help to inform a unique business strategy that works for you.

Do a quick SWOT analysis: A SWOT analysis is used to evaluate your business's Strengths, Weaknesses, Opportunities, and Threats. Like with your finances, an awareness and understanding of your situation is necessary for your strategic planning and will open your eyes to what you're working with—and what's working against you.

- **Strengths** refer to the things at which you excel, and the assets and advantages you might have over your competitors. Examples include an assisting background in your genre, a great mentor, unique skills, or niche knowledge.
- **Weaknesses** refer to things upon which you can improve and that you may struggle with professionally. Examples include a lack of industry knowledge, an insufficient professional network, or ineffective marketing.
- **Opportunities** refer to external factors you can potentially exploit to your advantage. Examples include trends, upcoming events (for event photographers or photojournalists), or new and untapped markets.
- **Threats** include challenges, limitations, and restrictions you can foresee. Examples include competitors, a poor economy, or debt and cash-flow problems.

**Define Your
Idea of Success**

What's your endgame?
What does having
"made it" look like
to you? There is no
one single prototype
of the successful
photographer. Some
won't be happy until
they're shooting
multiple editorial
and commercial
campaigns a year
and have created
a brand around
themselves. Others
are happy simply
having the freedom
to take landscape
shots and get paid
regularly for it.
Sometimes it's about
being recognized as
a master and an artist;
other times, it's simply
a numbers game and
profit trumps all. No
one idea of success is
wrong; it's all about
personal preference.
Find out what your
pie-in-the-sky goal is,
write it down, and use
the resources in this
book (and all around
you) to help you
get there.

Research your ideal clients. So you've decided on your specialty, and know the kind of work you want to get, and from whom (see Find a Specialty, page 80). Now it's time to get really specific. If your specialty is fashion photography and you want to get magazine editorial work, then outline exactly which magazines you want to work for. Don't limit yourself to the major fashion ones; smaller, indie magazines are more likely to work with emerging photographers and are a great stepping-stone. (See Getting Work, page 30). Similarly, if your specialty is commercial photography, outline the exact brands you want to work with, find out what agencies they represented by and study their campaigns. By knowing the specific clients you're targeting, you'll be able to apply marketing and advertising strategies more narrowly and effectively. (See Marketing & Advertising, Chapter 6.)

If you don't have specific clients in mind, then at least try to carve out a niche for yourself within your genre. Having a niche can be more rewarding and profitable than trying to own the entire genre (portrait photography, for example, can be narrowed down to head shots, child portraiture, or family portraiture). Remember, this isn't set in stone—your business plan can change many times throughout the course of your career. The most important thing initially is to have goals that will continually push you forward.

Know your competitors: Your competitors aren't exactly your enemies, but keep them close anyway. Find out as much about other similar photography businesses already working in your genre. Study the clients with whom they've worked, what they've been commissioned, and their own individual niches. You certainly shouldn't attempt to shadow their careers or copy their work, but draw inspiration from their successes. Cherry-pick what you like and don't like about their business, the way they deal with clients, and the methods and means by which they have "come up." See what's worked for them, and what hasn't—and then learn from that. It's only by studying and understanding your competitors that you can strategize ways of standing out from them.

MARKETING & ADVERTISING

Marketing and advertising—essentially, selling your services—are two of a working photographer's most despised tasks. But combined, they are the backbone of every successful photographer; without them, you risk becoming irrelevant or even nonexistent in the eyes of the photography industry. Marketing and advertising can be challenging and tedious, but it's a necessary means of attracting new clients, keeping current clients, and growing your business. The landscape has shifted so that photographic skill alone is not nearly enough— to survive in this competitive digital age, you must also be an intelligent and aggressive salesperson, across all platforms.

Author Note
If you're concerned that you're limiting yourself, the truth is that having a strong, recognizable brand makes it easier for potential client to decide to hire you— because they already know exactly what they can expect.

CREATE YOUR BRAND

To begin with, you need a brand—your distinct style, your "thing," that special look or feel apparent in everything you shoot that makes it uniquely you. It's beyond a specialty or niche, though these certainly help to inform your brand. It's more of a way of powerfully distinguishing who you are and why you are different from the next commercial photographer, or the next family portrait photographer, or the next fashion editorial photographer. (Photographers Annie Leibovitz, Steven Klein, and Terry Richardson are all famous for their distinct brands.) Having a brand also makes it easier for you to narrow your images down into a strong, tight portfolio.

"It's important to have an individual brand or look that sets you apart from the other competitors and masses out there. If you possess and represent an individual style, you have a higher chance of a potential client seeking you out based on the look and needs they're trying to connect with."

AMANDA COOPER
ART DIRECTOR

"It's a misconception that an elaborate promo will get you any more work than a postcard. You may get more attention from your peers and on photo blogs, but in the end, all an art producer or photo editor cares about is the photography.
I will say that attention to detail in the printing, construction, and care with which the promo is made can add to the impression that you are a professional, so it's not all about the images, but the most elaborate promo with poor quality photography will get chucked in the trash just as quickly as anything else."

ROB HAGGART
FORMER PHOTO EDITOR & FOUNDER,
APHOTOEDITOR.COM

"Getting commissions as a professional photographer isn't just about pure art and talent anymore—it's that, but so much more. You need to be smart and marketing-savvy; you need to create your own opportunities, chase the right people, know how to use social media, and think cleverly about ways to attract attention amid the sheer number of hungry photographers out there. It's quite challenging, but you sort of always need to be thinking about all of those elements."

AMANDA COOPER
ART DIRECTOR

PROMOTIONAL MATERIAL

The brand you create for yourself strongly influences the promotional materials that you will need to circulate as part of your marketing efforts. Before creating anything listed below, it's wise to consult a graphic designer who will examine your brand and collaborate with you to create a consistent, multi-platform "branding" strategy that includes logo design, business cards, a website and portfolio, print promos, and social media.

Website & online portfolio: In this digital age, your website and online portfolio are the most powerful promotional tools you have (see Photography in the Digital Age, Chapter 7). Having a professional-looking website with great search engine optimization (SEO), user-friendly navigation, and a narrowly edited portfolio is mandatory for any photography business today (see Tips for a Solid Portfolio, page 94).

Print promos: There's a debate currently happening regarding the effectiveness and relevance of traditional printed promotional materials mailed to potential clients. An increasing number of advertising agencies no longer accept mailed print promos from photographers for reasons such as eco-awareness and the sheer volume of promos received daily. Because of their perceived outdatedness, many

photographers have resorted to flashy and expensive gimmicks (as opposed to a postcard or flyer) to get the attention of clients. But unless there is evidence that these pricey gimmicks actually translate into real-life jobs, simple, classic print promos aren't worth discounting just yet; they are still a way of getting your name and brand out there, as rone part of a wider marketing campaign.

Email campaigns: Getting a subscription to an international industry database (Agency Access has a great one) and creating targeted email campaigns is another powerful way to market yourself. Email campaign managers like Agency Access, MailChimp, and Constant Contact not only get you into the inboxes of potential clients, they provide you with crucial data on who views your campaigns and who clicks through to your website and portfolio. This information narrows the field and allows you to directly target those who have already shown interest in your work.

Social media: Social media is not generally considered promotional material per se, but it is just as valuable a tool as a great website or a solid print promo. Social media channels like Facebook, Instagram, Tumblr, and Twitter are powerful and instantaneous means of promoting your work. (See Your Digital Presence, page 174.)

"It's been proven that email promotions will help you generate work. They allow you to stay in front of clients, drive traffic to your site, and keep current clients informed on your latest projects, among other things. However, they are the icing on the cake of your entire marketing campaign."

AMANDA SOSA STONE
CREATIVE CONSULTANT

Hit the Streets!
No email campaign or promo is as effective as picking up the phone or emailing the clients or ad agencies with whom you want to work (see Networking, page 96). Use industry databases and social media to find out the numbers or emails of art producers, art directors, and creative directors. Ask if you can drop into their office and show your portfolio—be bold about it. These short meet-and-greets might not land you a job straight away, but once they've met you in person and gotten a sense of who you are, you'll come to mind when they need a photographer in the future.

RESOURCES

Marketing and advertising might feel like an overwhelming task, but the following resources exist to make it a little easier.

Industry database subscriptions: As mentioned in the previous section, subscribing to an industry database can be a significant benefit to your business. Having access to what is essentially a phone and e-mail directory of creative industry professionals saves you from the laborious and time-consuming task of having to find their contact details on your own. Agency Access offers a terrific, comprehensive creative buyers database that is updated regularly.

Photo-industry consultants: If you struggle to examine your work objectively, or simply need more guidance, it's a good idea to call in the services of a photo-industry consultant. Photo consultants can review your portfolio, give you feedback, and edit it to better appeal to your target clients. If you're just starting out, a consultant can help you to cement your brand and vision (see Create Your Brand, page 150).

FINANCES

You might be a creative, but there's no excuse for being financially illiterate when it comes to your business. Knowing how to discuss money with clients, correctly bill and invoice, track expenses, and forecast revenue isn't just a good idea—it's essential to your photography business. Here's a basic guide to what you should know.

YOUR CREATIVE FEE

The first money question that will probably come to mind is, "How much do I get paid?" Depending on your specialty, the nature of the job, the client you're working for, the country you're working in, and your own experience level, that figure will vary—there is no standard industry rate across the board that I can quote here. Your national or local photography organization (see Join a Photo Organization, page 20) will be a helpful resource for gauging your fee for specific shoots, as will many forums and articles regarding pricing on websites like PhotoShelter, Fstoppers, APhotoEditor, and A Wonderful Machine. Invoicing programs like Blinkbid and ShootQ also offer creative fee estimates you can go by. A trusted colleague or mentor (see Find a Mentor, page 22) will also be able to advise on real world rates.

Advice for Photo Assistants on Fees:
Before accepting any assignment, make sure you ask the money questions first: What are the rates for this job? Is there OT (overtime after 10 hours)? Is it advertising or editorial? The broadly typical US-dollar rates are as follows:

Magazine editorials:
$250 for a ten-hour day
Advertising/commercial:
$350 for a ten-hour day
Regular first assistant:
$400 for a ten-hour day
Digital tech:
$500 a day

After ten hours, time-and-a-half is the standard OT rate.

Always, always
ensure you've received
an advance or deposit
and a contract before
even putting a client
down in your calendar.
Many photographers
have been burned by
booking and planning
a shoot before a client
has put their money
where their mouth is.

BUDGETS & ESTIMATES

Once you get booked for a shoot—whether it's commercial, editorial, event, or portrait—your client will have a budget. What elements fall under that budget depend on the specifics of the shoot, but it will likely include your creative fee, the location fee, and the human resources required to make the shoot happen (see Who's On Set?, page 117). It should also include licensing fees, which take into consideration how, where, and for how long the images will be used by your client. Again, there is no standard industry rate for these across the board—depending on the nature of the images and your client's use for them, these fees might vary wildly and it's best to consult online resources, photo organizations, and invoicing programs like Blinkbid and ShootQ to help you determine these specific figures.

In commercial shoots, you'll generally be asked to put together an estimate for the shoot—that is, a breakdown of how much you'll actually spend for the shoot, all factors considered. This typically happens after the budget has been determined, so that you have a guideline of how much you can spend. But in certain cases—like in the instance that several photographers are bidding on one commercial job—you might have to put together an estimate without one. This is more challenging, but also offers you more freedom to pitch resources and ideas you wouldn't normally.

Once your estimate has been approved, you should typically ask for an advance, particularly for bigger-budget shoots (y ou won't generally get an advance for editorials and smaller shoots). The advance is a fraction of the budget arbitrarily determined by the client, and will generally be enough money to get the production started— e.g. booking locations, equipment, etc.—usually with the help of a producer.

Author Note
A contract is a 100% necessary document that holds both parties accountable to their responsibilities, protects you and your business, and ensures you get paid—so take it seriously. If a potential client shies away from putting your deal in writing, consider that a big red flag.

CONTRACTS

Before any job, a contract must be signed by both photographer and client that outlines a description of services, copyright and licensing details, payment terms, and all other pertinent parts of your agreement that should be secured in writing.

For bigger-budget commercial productions commissioned by advertising agencies or large corporations, you can expect a contract to be sent to you. However, for smaller productions or events and portrait gigs, you will most likely need to draft up your own contract to send to the client before the job. The way your contract will look is dependent on your photography specialty and the nature of the job. You can download free templates from your local photography organization's website, but, to be safe, have a lawyer create a boilerplate contract for you that you can customize for each new client.

Accounts

GET ORGANIZED

Constantly winging your finances is a recipe for disaster. Open up a business account, keep an eye on your expenditure, and ensure all your bills, invoices, and receipts are documented and categorized properly. Continuous, hawk-eyed monitoring of your daily, weekly, and monthly finances (and keeping the documents to back it all up) will keep you in line.

Open a business account: Having a separate bank account and credit card for strictly business-related expenses will help you distinguish easily between charges. You'll still need to keep receipts and monitor expenses (see the next point); this just simplifies the process for you. It also makes life a lot easier should you ever get audited during tax time. (Should you choose to incorporate your business, it's required by law that you have a separate business bank account.)

Track your business expenses: You can keep it analog and track everything you spend on your business via pen and paper—to each their own—but it's a good idea to invest in business-accounting software like QuickBooks, Sage 50, FreshBooks, Xero, or InDinero. These programs make it infinitely easier to keep an eye on the health of your business, put together financial statements, and send detailed data to your accountant come tax time.

Author Note
It may well seem tedious when you start budgeting out your entire life down to the decimal point, but you'll be surprised how quickly this will become second nature, and the benefits make it more than worthwhile.

Budgeting: Sadly, the term "budgeting" has a negative connotation and is often associated with deprivation. Naturally, you should always consider where you can cut costs (e.g., with all the cheap, web-based entertainment streaming programs these days, do you really need that $90-per-month cable subscription?). But it mainly means being smart with your money by properly allocating your funds. The easiest method is to break it down via percentage—e.g., 10% of your monthly take-home pay is set aside for savings, 25% for rent, 10% for food, 5% for health, 10% for transportation, and so on. Having your funds properly allocated will ensure that you cover all your bases, all the time, and never fall short.

Keep your receipts: As mentioned earlier, scanned copies of your production-expense receipts should accompany every invoice, but it's also important to keep track of your receipts for your own records and for tax purposes. You can keep the originals in a folder, or even better, use digital receipt-keeping software like Shoeboxed, NeatReceipts, or Expensify. Some business-accounting software like QuickBooks also allow you to scan and store business receipts.

HIRE A BUSINESS ACCOUNTANT

Having a business accountant, specifically one that works with freelancers, self-employed individuals, and small business owners, will help you make educated financial decisions regarding your photography business. If you don't quite have enough money to take on a business accountant at the beginning, it's still a good idea to schedule a one-off appointment to discuss a plan and help you set the overall financial tone for your business going forward. For starters, a business accountant can help you work out how much to set aside for taxes, establish your monthly take-home pay, find out where you can cut costs, and teach you how to forecast revenue. At the very least, they'll be able to point out the obvious problems with how you're currently operating, so that you're not scraping by from paycheck to paycheck (the starving-artist thing is not cool). Even if you're already on top of your finances, an accountant can help you to maximize profitability and invest in your future.

A Note on Taxes
Filing taxes as a freelancer differs greatly from country to country. For exact information on filing taxes in your country, please consult a local business accountant that works with freelancers, self-employed individuals, and small business owners. Better to be safe than sorry here.

MULTIPLE INCOME STREAMS

It's never advisable to put all your eggs in one basket, and that's especially true in the modern-day photo industry. Many editorial photographers today are no longer able support themselves by shooting for magazines alone, unlike ten years ago. There is increased competition, tighter budgets, and, many would argue, decreased opportunity across all genres. That said, it's wise for all photographers these days to have a diversified income stream. Having other revenue trickling in regularly from sources outside your photographic services is in your best financial interest. What this looks like will differ greatly depending on your specialty and individual brand, but some examples of other income streams might be:

Selling products: Whether fine art, wedding, or portraiture, selling photo prints has long been an additional income stream for many photographers to accompany their services. In this digital age, "selling prints" now extends to high-res digital images, online galleries, DVDs, and even personalized, on-demand books and albums. Depending on your genre, your photographs might also lend well to calendars, postcards, posters, and other printed matter.

"This industry now just does not have enough work to support as many photographers as it once did. You might need a mix of different shooting gigs, plus publishing, stock, book publishing, corporate work, consulting—just some blend, so that when one revenue stream dwindles, the others can help take up the slack."

ROBERT WRIGHT
EDITORIAL & PORTRAIT PHOTOGRAPHER

Author Note
These are just a
handful of ways
you can diversify your
income stream, and
not all of these will
necessarily work for
you. But if you think
outside the box and
maintain a healthy
entrepreneurial
mindset, the
possibilities really
are endless.

Blogging: Start your own photography blog and earn income from advertisements, sponsors, and affiliated links. You can also blog for more established photography blogs and get paid on a per-article basis.

Private assignments: If you're a commercial or editorial photographer, you might consider shooting events, private functions, or portraits on the side. You don't necessarily have to incorporate this work into your portfolio if it deviates from your brand, but it's another viable source of income. Corporate portraiture can be particularly lucrative.

Photographic services: You might consider offering services such as digitization, retouching, printing, or publishing as a side business.

Training: Depending on your level of experience, you could consider conducting photography training sessions or tutorials for beginners at your local photography studio or even online. YouTube has become an extremely lucrative way of making additional income via ads, provided you've built up a large following. You should jump on any available opportunity to leverage your photographic knowledge for additional income.

Stock images: Apply to be a contributor to a stock photo agency and collect commissions or royalties every time your images are used.

PHOTOGRAPHY
IN THE DIGITAL AGE

SEVEN

Author Note
Of course, there's a flip side to this era of incredible innovation. The reproducibility of digital images, and the countless platforms that facilitate their dissemination have made current attitudes toward copyright dangerously cavalier. And while there have never been more pro photographers than there are today, some have argued that the quality of photography across the board has suffered because of it. Some lament that the art of photography has diminished, while others defend that it's simply changed. In my experience, it's far more productive to embrace the latter perspective—and to keep up the pace.

Professional photographic equipment has never been cheaper, publishing and showcasing images across multiple platforms has never been easier. Photography-related informational resources, technical tutorials, and advice forums can all be accessed with a click. The sheer number of people looking at and for pictures is completely unprecedented and the photography industry has never been more popular or accessible.

No matter how you look at it, it's an interesting time for photography. If you put aside the anxiety that surrounds the survival of the medium at its most traditional, you could argue that its experiencing an exciting new beginning. The modern-day photographer must be savvy and multi-skilled; they must be a website expert, a blogger, a social media master, a marketing pro. They must know how to specialize and then stand out in a saturated market, promote their images while protecting themselves against copyright infringement. They must network harder than ever and be more creative, take more risks, and create their own opportunities instead of waiting for them to appear. Because of all the noise, content, and congestion, photographers have never had to push themselves harder creatively. It's challenging, and exciting.

YOUR DIGITAL PRESENCE

The Yellow Pages are dead, replaced instead by the powerful digital trifecta that is a website, blog, and social-media presence. In this day and age, if you don't exist online, you don't exist at all—and this is particularly true for businesses. Take it seriously, and you'll be surprised, and pleased, at how a strong digital presence can translate directly into real-world success.

> "Before you even start, an impressive website is an absolute must. It is necessary for photographers. Without it, you have no chance at all."
>
> **PETER "POBY" POBYJPICZ**
> COMMERCIAL PHOTOGRAPHER

CREATE A KILLER WEBSITE

Your website and online portfolio are your most powerful marketing tools (see Marketing & Advertising, page 150) so you need to ensure they both look flawless. That said, you don't need to shell out thousands for a web developer to custom-build a fancy website from scratch—Squarespace, PhotoFolio, Wordpress, and Cargo Collective are cost-effective website builders and hosting services that can help you create a site that's beautiful, functional, and professional. Here are some things to keep in mind when creating your website.

DEMETRIUS FORDHAM

DO...

Have easy & intuitive navigation: Don't make it hard for people to get around your site. Getting to your portfolio should take one or two clicks at most, so create good navigation links. Ensure that core pages—like your Contact page, About page, and portfolio—are easily visible from the homepage navigation bar and not hidden in navigation drop-downs or within other pages.

Use SEO: Search Engine Optimization helps to ensure that your site is seen by potential clients during searches, by incorporating search-engine-friendly elements into your website. It involves optimizing your site with the right search terms via relevant, keyword-rich content, correct keyword placement, back links, alt tags on images, and getting listed on local search engines like Google+ Local, among other things. If the thought of SEO only makes you shudder, don't worry—there are many SEO and coding experts out there who can do it for you.

CHAPTER 7 | PHOTOGRAPHY IN THE DIGITAL AGE

Analytics
Google Analytics is a free tool that gives you loads of valuable information about visitors to your site. These comprehensive stats will help you concentrate on the important parts of your website, and improve the overall experience of the site.

Integrate social media: It is vital to integrate social media into your website. Social-media channels like Instagram, Facebook, Twitter, and Tumblr are all platforms for showcasing your work, so it makes sense to promote them every chance you get. Your professional website is also the ideal place to tie together all of your social-media accounts (your Contact section is a good place for these links).

Have a well-organized portfolio or gallery:
Don't just throw all the photos you've ever taken onto your website and hope that clients scroll through until they find what they're looking for. Separate your work into distinct galleries or portfolios based on genre—e.g., fashion, beauty, editorial, portraiture, or whatever makes sense to you. Your website should never look like one massive image dump.

Use web-optimized photos: This tip might seem commonsensical, but the number of photographers guilty of posting poor-quality images to their site is surprisingly high. Whether it's a newbie mistake or an effort to prevent unauthorized usage, there's no faster way to appear amateur and unprofessional. It's critical to use high-res photos on your website! 900×1500 pixels at 72ppi will look good on most monitors, and will still load relatively fast.

Have e-commerce capabilities: If selling prints, stock, or any kind of product is part of your hustle, then make sure your website is actually built for it. Again, you don't need a web developer to achieve this—Squarespace and other website builders let you add fully integrated e-commerce capabilities into your site, and allow you to accept instant payments.

DON'T...

Use Adobe Flash: Flash might make your site look amazing, but it can also make it slow and difficult to load. Also, search engines can't read text inside a Flash-based site (your site will just read as a large blank page) so you'll risk a low search ranking. Just avoid it; you didn't need that video-montage opener anyway.

Have background music: I get that you want to set the tone and mood for your website. But do it through your images and website design, not through music. It also drains bandwidth, might get you in trouble with music copyright (especially embarrassing for a fellow artist) and simply doesn't come across as professional.

Have a slow-loading website: It's simple: if your website takes forever to load, people will get bored and leave. Search engines also rank you lower for having a slow website. (Not having Flash is a good start.)

START BLOGGING

If you're a business with a website—regardless of size—chances are, you'll also have a blog connected to it. That's because businesses have realized the benefits of their brand having a relatable "voice." Yeah, I get it—you have absolutely no desire to write. But it's not all about writing! Many visual artists blog pictures that they wouldn't necessarily add to their portfolio, but that are still beautiful enough to share. Here are some other reasons you should consider blogging:

Showcasing new work: Blogging is a great way to announce that you have added new images to your portfolio. It doesn't need to be an essay every time (in fact it shouldn't be); each post can simply be a few lines describing your new work, a little about how and where it was shot, and then your tear sheets or images. Don't forget to share the love and link out to your updated portfolio and the original site on which your images have been published, if online.

Keeping it fresh & relevant: Portfolio sites have a tendency to feel stagnant, particularly as many photographers neglect to update them regularly. Posting short weekly blogs on where you are, what you're doing, and projects you're excited about is a great way to keep your site feeling continuously new and fresh, and helps keep clients interested.

Improving SEO: It's true—blogging helps boost your SEO. Updating your blog with frequent and keyword-rich content helps your site inch closer and closer to the top of search rankings.

Developing a personal voice: Sure, your photos are beautiful, but people like to know the person with whom they're working. In this competitive and cutthroat digital age, raw talent isn't enough—you need to find and seize other ways of standing out. Developing a unique personal voice via blogging is one of them.

GET SOCIAL-MEDIA SAVVY

The term "social media" might conjure images of drunken colleagues at holiday parties, cat videos, and vintage-filter sunsets (thank you, Instagram). But it's a bandwagon you need to hop on, business-wise, if you haven't already. Social media is an excellent way to showcase your work, increase your brand presence, reach new audiences, and engage with others in the photo industry across many different platforms. You don't need to jump on all of them, but each channel offers its own audience and distinctive kind of exposure that can be extremely beneficial to your business.

Author Note
Make sure you've set
up your page to notify
you of any and all
comments and activity,
so that you can swiftly
respond to comments
and questions—
engaging with your
fans is essential.

Facebook: Set up an official business page on Facebook that's separate from your personal page. It should be titled with the name of your business, and be consistent with your business' branding (see Create Your Brand, page 150). Your Facebook page should be regularly updated with new work, old work, and blog posts, although posts should be limited to once a day to avoid congesting followers' feeds with your work. Be very selective about the photographs you upload to Facebook (save the iPhoneography for Instagram) and don't post for the sake of posting; it will only lower brand value. It's also a good idea to explore paid Facebook advertising as a way of increasing exposure (you can start promoting posted content for as little as $5).

Facebook

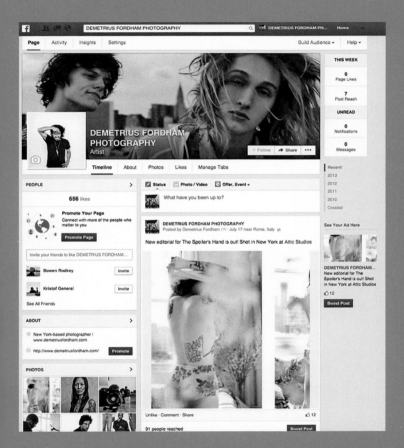

Author Note
The massive reach of Instagram has put it on the radar of some very big clients, who will pay top dollar for you to share photos of their product, service, or destination—provided you have a sizeable (i.e., massive) number of followers. Getting such a large audience is a lofty goal, but one that pays for itself along the way in terms of getting your brand out there.

Instagram: There's an ongoing debate about whether Instagram should be used by professional photographers, or if it's better left to filter-happy amateurs—basically whether it hurts or helps the photo industry at large. Whatever side of the debate you're on, you can't deny Instagram's reach or power—so, from a business perspective, you may as well leverage it. If you're not comfortable posting work from your portfolio because of Instagram's terms of use, you should still consider using it to post behind-the-scenes shots, promo material, or shots from work-related travels. Think of it as merely another image-driven way of increasing your brand presence and building an audience. Remember that everyone is on Instagram these days—including photo editors, art directors, and endless potential clients.

Instagram

"It's very important to be active on social media. Photo editors and art producers are reading blogs; they're on Facebook, Instagram, and Twitter. I just wouldn't bet the farm on any one method for getting noticed."

ROB HAGGART
FORMER PHOTO EDITOR & FOUNDER, APHOTOEDITOR.COM

Twitter: Twitter might not be as visual as Facebook or Instagram, but it doesn't mean it's any less effective for promoting your photography business. It's not all about showcasing your work on every possible channel, it's about increasing brand presence and audience. Unlike Facebook and Instagram, which are largely dedicated to image sharing, Twitter is a platform designed for finding and sharing news, tutorials, and other informational resources useful for photographers. And that's the beauty of it—by finding, sharing, and re-tweeting relevant content, you're able to connect with countless others in the photo community who will, in turn, be organically exposed to your brand.

Tumblr & Pinterest: Tumblr and Pinterest are as loathed by professional photographers as Instagram, if not more; both channels make it even easier to share/reblog/repin images without credit. (This is not acceptable, and if your copyright is violated, you should flag it to each site's support team; Tumblr support is particularly swift at handling copyright issues.) A much easier way to cover yourself, though, is to watermark all of the images you upload to each of these sites. Having the name of your photography business and a link to your website on each image means more eyeballs to your site.

"Photographers that grew up downloading free content don't realize how powerful copyright can be and how successful it has been to keep the US arts community vibrant. It allowed me to feed my family, buy a house, put my kid through college, and produce my documentary book projects. Young photographers need to learn about copyright and fight for their rights. The idea that content should be free is a lovely idealistic one, but artists can't survive on free. Your pictures should be valued."

DOUG MENUEZ
COMMERCIAL &
DOCUMENTARY
PHOTOGRAPHER

PROTECT COPYRIGHT

As mentioned in the introduction to this chapter, technology has resulted in dangerously cavalier attitudes toward copyright. The sharing of uncredited photos, and the posting of credited photos without permission, has simply become the norm. This is not okay: your livelihood depends on being paid for your pictures and theft should not be tolerated. Contact your local photography organization for information on copyright seminars and lectures. In the meantime, here's how you can protect your work:

Use copyright notices: Embed a copyright notice in the bottom corner of every photo you upload. An official copyright notice will have a copyright symbol, the year your work was published and your name (e.g., © 2015 Joel Canfield Photography). The notice serves as a reminder that the work is protected, and it is illegal for someone to remove the notice and use it without authorization.

Encode

Use photo watermarks: If you're worried that a watermark might distract from your photo, use Digimarc or similar software. Digimarc will digitally encode the watermark so that it can't be seen on the photo, but is detectable to computers. It essentially allows you to track your work across the web and see if any copyright infringements have taken place.

Register your copyrights: In the United States, you can do this via the U.S. Copyright Office's online registration system, eCO, the Electronic Copyright Office. You can register individual photos, or batches of photos at a time. Registering your work ensures that if your work has been stolen, you'll be eligible for statutory damages of up to $150,000.

Make copying difficult: The simplest way to do this is to disable right-clicking capabilities—this way, people can't simply copy and save your image to their own computer.

©2014 Demetrius Fordham

CHAPTER 7 | PHOTOGRAPHY IN THE DIGITAL AGE

EIGHT

SURVIVING IN THE INDUSTRY

> The only way to survive and thrive as a photographer is to first figure out what you are passionate about and what you see that no one else does. Refine that vision into a powerful, tight portfolio that is not for everyone, and combine it with smart, long-term business planning. Keep in mind that you probably will fail—but without failure, you'll never hit it out of the park, either."

DOUG MENUEZ
COMMERCIAL &
DOCUMENTARY
PHOTOGRAPHER

Working in this crazy industry is one thing—but lasting in it is a separate challenge altogether. A business plan, financial strategy, strong digital presence, and solid marketing tactics might get you from job to job, but achieving career longevity requires an additional set of skills paired with dogged commitment.

One of the key skills for surviving as a photographer in the long run is developing a thick skin and a healthy attitude toward failure and rejection. Though that's applicable to every career, the competitive and cutthroat nature of this industry calls for a higher level of resilience; without it, you can swiftly undermine your own progress. Another skill is learning how to forge a unique path to your own "end game" via personal projects and outside-the-box thinking. It's also recognizing that to be truly successful as a photographer, you can't go it alone: there's more teamwork involved than you might think. On top of all that, every successful photographer must learn how to actively prevent career burnout by setting boundaries and working toward a work/life balance. (I never said this photography thing was easy!) The lessons offered in this final chapter will help build upon the essential skills taught in previous chapters, and will offer advice from experts on how to survive and thrive in the industry once you're in it.

HOW TO MAKE IT

Talent, education, networks, and business savvy are important, but what's crucial to the success and career longevity of a photographer is his or her ability to do the following:

FIND YOUR OWN PATH

As explained in Chapter Five (see Define Your Idea of Success, page 148), having "made it" as a photographer will look different to each individual based on their chosen genre, their values, and their priorities. Consequently, the path to each individual's end game will look different, too, so it's important not to view another successful photographer's path as a strict roadmap. Though having a mentor is invaluable (see Find a Mentor, page 22), you should use their career as a source of inspiration and education rather than trying to mirror or reproduce it. The mistake many emerging photographers make is to try and model one's work and style after the photographers they admire, out of a lack of confidence in their own creative abilities. But remember: you're bringing a unique set of skills, talent, and influences to the table, so work to develop these.

SHOOT PERSONAL PROJECTS

Once the commissioned work starts rolling in, it's easy to get caught up in it—after all, the point of being a photographer is getting paid to shoot, right? But if you want to avoid early career burnout and keep the love of photography alive,

> "Don't be afraid of niche areas you're interested in. There's this amazing work being done by a guy shooting dogs jumping in pools that's getting lots of attention. It's all about finding your own thing that's all yours, that you are passionate about, and just shooting like hell."
>
> **DOUG MENUEZ**
> COMMERCIAL &
> DOCUMENTARY
> PHOTOGRAPHER

it's important to have your own personal projects on the side. There should always be something you want to shoot for the sake of shooting rather than for a paycheck. It doesn't matter if it's not trendy, or it doesn't fit into a clear-cut genre, or is seemingly unmarketable. Be on constant lookout for subjects or ideas that challenge, excite, and scare you. This kind of passion will shine through your images and can potentially draw attention to your work. Even if it doesn't, you'll still have photographs that you're proud of, that can potentially add depth and dimension to your existing body of work.

EMBRACE REJECTION

No matter how well prepared you are, the reality is that things may not go your way at some point, or several points, throughout your career. You'll bid on jobs that you won't get; you'll produce work that doesn't meet a client's expectations, for reasons beyond your control; you'll cold call, email, reach out for meetings, and stick your neck out only to face another "no" or no response at all. Rejection is a reality in this industry that cannot be avoided, and the sooner you accept it as an inevitable part of your professional career, the faster you can move on and find your next "yes." Apply the same principles used in Troubleshooting (page 124).

"You've got to be willing to go through hard times and rejection and failure in order to succeed as a photographer. When you fail, just get up and start again. It's actually that simple."

PETER "POBY"
POBYJPICZ
COMMERCIAL
PHOTOGRAPHER

As you grow professionally, this will extend to a team that will support and help you progress in your career. Though this is viewed as a highly self-oriented career, the reality is that you will work with other people in some capacity for most projects. With that in mind, it's important to build a team around you that you trust. As you progress throughout your career, consider finding a supportive agent who "gets" your work and has your best interests in mind, a hyper-organized studio manager, a reliable first assistant (this is key!), and an excellent accountant or business manager. It's also a good idea to have other photographers as friends, not just for career advancement (see Networking, page 96) but also as a supportive peer network.

You can also use rejection to your advantage by exploring the reasons why a potential client did not want to work with you. If they didn't provide a definitive reason, then don't be afraid to seek it: ask them, respectfully, why you were unsuccessful in this instance, and what you could have done to better your chances. Did certain images in your portfolio work against you? Was it a negative review from a previous client that had made its rounds? Was it simply a lack of experience and previous work, or perhaps a lack of a specific kind of work? There is so much knowledge to be gleaned from your apparent "failures" or rejections; be thankful for the invaluable lessons they will teach.

PREVENT BURNOUT

Photography is not a nine-to-five job that you can "switch off" once you leave the office. You'll most likely find yourself working on weeknights, weekends, and even holidays (particularly event photographers or wedding photographers). You may live and breathe photography, but at some point, you need to give it a rest. It's particularly important in this line of work to achieve a work/life balance by doing the following:

"I adhere to a schedule. I try to not work between 6–8pm. I do my old-man routine and make dinner and watch the news. I also don't answer emails after 6pm; my clients should not expect to have me around the clock. It's one part of the 'always on' culture that I try to avoid."

ROBERT WRIGHT
EDITORIAL & PORTRAIT
PHOTOGRAPHER

Do something (at least) once a week that's not remotely photography-related: Go rock climbing, set aside time to read a novel, do yoga, take a boxing class, or go fishing. These types of distractions will allow you to return to your work refreshed and rejuvenated.

Spend quality time with family or friends: Simply be around people who love and support you, and be completely present during that time: turn off your cellphone, or better yet, leave it at home.

Set boundaries and learn to say No: It might be tempting, but don't take every job that comes your way; if you're lucky enough to be bombarded with work, then pick only the ones that will further your career. Do not overextend yourself by working back-to-back jobs. It's not healthy or sustainable.

Adopt healthy habits: Eat well, exercise, and sleep at least six hours a night—especially while on the job.

Nurture your creative side: Flexing your creative muscles keeps you excited and challenged, and helps fight burnout—whether you're being creative with your photography (see Shoot Personal Projects, page 194), or through other avenues like painting, cooking, or writing.

THE TEN COMMANDMENTS

According to a select panel of photographers and experts, this is how to survive and succeed in the photography industry in ten simple directives.

1. Be humble: "As an artist, you never stop paying your dues. Challenge yourself, constantly, to grow and keep learning, even at 80. Try to maintain a beginner's mind, open to new ideas and solutions. Don't pretend you know everything—stay open-minded and humble no matter how successful you become."

DOUG MENUEZ
COMMERCIAL &
DOCUMENTARY
PHOTOGRAPHER

2. Have a good attitude: "The industry seems to spawn some divas and huge egos, of the 'legends-in-their-own-mind' variety. In my experience, it eventually catches up with them. An art buyer once told me that there are many photographers that potentially can do any given job, and, all things being equal, they'll choose the one with the best attitude and most simpatico personality. The one who contributes yet listens, is receptive to ideas, and is basically a team player."

ELLEN ERWITT
OWNER/PRODUCER,
BIG SPLASH
PRODUCTIONS

3. Get business-savvy: "Having a clear idea about the direction you want your photography business to go in the coming years, and creating a strong business plan that's adaptable to change, is crucial to the success of any photographer."

PETER "POBY" POBYJPICZ
COMMERCIAL
PHOTOGRAPHER

4. Network: "People hire the people they trust and connect with. That doesn't mean that having the right contacts will necessarily trump talent, but you can't deny the importance of 'who you know' in an industry where traditional opportunities are so limited."

DOUG MENUEZ
COMMERCIAL &
DOCUMENTARY
PHOTOGRAPHER

5. Create a distinct brand: "It's necessary for an emerging photographer to distinguish their unique brand. It should be reflected in their website, the final delivery of the work, and everything in between. It's important for an artist to be aware of how they want to be perceived."

AMANDA SOSA STONE
CREATIVE CONSULTANT

6. Be bold: "Getting out there is key. You can't sit at home hoping the phone will ring if you don't show your face and aren't proactive. Make calls to the clients you want to have in order to get appointments, and have a face-to-face meeting over your portfolio."

PETER "POBY" POBYJPICZ
COMMERCIAL
PHOTOGRAPHER

7. Get your money right, ASAP: "It's a terribly difficult time to make a living with photography. Don't squander the time where you have no mortgage or kids to raise; get your work out where it can be seen and hustle as hard as you can."

ROB HAGGART
FORMER PHOTO
EDITOR & FOUNDER,
APHOTOEDITOR.COM

8. Get online: "Photo editors and art producers are reading blogs; they're on Facebook, Instagram, and Twitter. I just wouldn't bet the farm on any one method for getting noticed."

ROB HAGGART
FORMER PHOTO
EDITOR & FOUNDER,
APHOTOEDITOR.COM

9. Stay passionate: "I want to feel, by looking at someone's images, that the work is truly a passion of the photographer, and not just a job. I want to hire a photographer who's in love with their craft, because they won't treat my job as if its 'just another job.'"

AMANDA COOPER
ART DIRECTOR

10. Be persistent: "Give yourself the space and trust to know that it will work out, in time, if you persist. You just can't quit."

ROBERT WRIGHT
EDITORIAL & PORTRAIT
PHOTOGRAPHER

Succeed

RESOURCES

CHAPTER 1: PAY YOUR DUES
FOR PHOTO ASSISTANTS
Find An Assistant, American Society
of Media Photographers:
http://asmp.org/find-an-assistant
Group for Assistants and Specialists
www.facebook.com/BeyondPhotoSchool
The Assistants' Handbook, Photo Shelter:
http://www.photoshelter.com/resources/
photo-assistant-handbook
Advice for Assistants, A Photo Editor:
http://www.aphotoeditor.com/advice-for-
photo-assistants-working-as-a-first-assistant

SELECT INTERNATIONAL EQUIPMENT RENTAL HOUSES & PHOTO STUDIOS
United States
Adorama: www.adoramarentals.com
Attic Studios: www.atticstudios.net
Barrow Lenses: www.borrowlenses.com
Industria Superstudio: www.industrianyc.com
Milk Studios: www.milkstudios.com
Pier 59 Studios: www.pier59studios.com
Samy's Camera: www.samys.com

Europe
Spring Studios (UK): www.springstudios.com
Loft Studios (UK): www.loftstudios.co.uk
Industria Superstudio (Italy):
www.superstudiogroup.com
Yorck Studio (Germany):
www.yorckstudio.com
Loft 506 (Germany):
www.scenelinestudios.com

WORKSHOPS & INTERNATIONAL PHOTO EXPOS
PhotoPlus Expo: www.photoplusexpo.com
Photokina: www.photokina.com
Photoville: www.photoville.com
Santa Fe Workshops:
www.santafeworkshops.com
Palm Springs Photo Festival
www.palmspringsphotofestival.com

PHOTO-INDUSTRY NEWS PUBLICATIONS & RESOURCES
A Photo Editor: www.aphotoeditor.com
Photo Shelter: www.photoshelter.com
PDN Online: www.pdnonline.com
Pro Photo: www.prophoto.com
Resource Magazine:
www.resourcemagonline.com
Joe Macnally: www.joemcnally.com
FStoppers: www.fstoppers.com
Feature Shoot www.featureshoot.com

CHAPTER 2: WHAT YOU'LL NEED
PROFESSIONAL EQUIPMENT
RETAILERS & RESOURCES
Nikon Pro Services: www.nikonpro.com
Canon Cameras Pro: www.cps.usa.canon.com
Pro Photo: www.prophoto.com
B&H Photo Video: www.bhphotovideo.com
Capture One Pro: www.phaseone.com
Adobe Photoshop: www.adobe.com

EDUCATIONAL RESOURCES & ONLINE TUTORIALS
Lynda: www.lynda.com
Creative Live: www.creativelive.com
Photo Focus: www.photofocus.com
SCU: www.skipcohenuniversity.com

PHOTOGRAPHER'S INSURERS
Tom C. Pickard & Co Inc.:
www.tcpinsurance.com
Taylor & Taylor Associates:
www.taylorinsurance.com

VENDOR DIRECTORY
Production Paradise:
www.productionparadise.com
411 Production Services:
www.variety411.com

INTERNATIONAL MODELING AGENCIES
Ford Models: www.models.fordmodels.com
Wilhelmina: www.wilhelmina.com

Marilyn Agency: www.marilynagency.com
DNA Model Management:
www.dnamodels.com
Elite Model Management:
www.elitemodel.com

PORTFOLIO PRINTERS
Adorama Pix: www.adoramapix.com
House of Portfolios:
www.houseofportfolios.com
White House Custom Color:
www.whcc.com

CHAPTER 3: WHAT YOU'LL NEED
PHOTO ORGANIZATIONS
American Society of Media Photographers:
www.asmp.org
American Photographic Artists:
www.apanational.org
Professional Photographers of America:
www.ppa.com

CHAPTER 4: ON THE JOB
TRAVEL RESOURCES
ATA Carnet: www.atacarnet.com
TSA: www.tsa.gov
U.S. Passports & International Travel:
www.travel.state.gov/content/passports/
english.html
Global Entry: www.cbp.gov/global-entry/
about
Travel Cards: www.comparecards.com

TRAVEL-CASE RETAILERS
Tenba Cases: www.tenba.com
Pelican Cases: www.pelicancases.com
Lowepro: www.lowepro.com

CHAPTER 5: THE BUSINESS
OF PHOTOGRAPHY
MARKETING & ADVERTISING SERVICES
Agency Access: www.agencyaccess.com
Wonderful Machine:
www.wonderfulmachine.com

Email Marketing
MailChimp www.mailchimp.com
Constant Contact
www.constantcontact.com
Myemma www.myemma.com
Vertical Response
www.verticalresponse.com
Mad Mimi www.madmimi.com

PORTFOLIO REVIEWS
United States
AIM Portfolio Review Series, New York:
www.nycfotoworks.com/portfolio-review
New York Portfolio Review:
www.lens.blogs.nytimes.com/category/
new-york-portfolio-review
Medium Festival Portfolio Reviews:
www.mediumsandiego.org/portfolio/portfolio-
reviews
SLOW Exposures Portfolio Review:
www.slowexposures.org/category/portfolio-
reviews
ACP Portfolio Review:
www.acpinfo.org/blog/category/acp-portfolio-
reviews
Powerhouse Portfolio Review:
www.powerhouseportfolioreview.com
PhotoNOLA Portfolio Review:
www.photonola.org/portfolio-review
Filter Festival Portfolio Review, Chicago:
www.filterfestival.com/portfolio-reviews-
2014
FotoFusion Portfolio Review:
http://www.fotofusion.org/pages/portfolio_
review.php
Fresh Look: A Portfolio Review www.
luciefoundation.org/education/freshlook/index.
php
Palm Springs Festival Portfolio Review:
www.palmspringsphotofestival.com/2014-
review
PhotoLucida Portfolio Review:
www.photolucida.org/portfolio-reviews
Review Santa Fe: www.visitcenter.org

New England Portfolio Reviews:
www.griffinmuseum.org/blog/new-england-portfolio-review
Look3 Festival of the Photograph Reviews:
www.look3.org

Europe
FORMAT13 Portfolio Reviews (UK):
www.formatfestival.com/events/portfolio-reviews
Fotofestival Mannheim_Ludwigshafen_ Heidelberg Portfolio Review (Germany)
www.fotofestival.info/en
PhotoIreland Portfolio Review (Ireland):
www.photoireland.org
Central European House of Photography International Portfolio Review (Slovakia):
www.sedf.sk/en/moph2014/portfolio14/117-the-international-portfolio-review-2014
Fine Arts Portfolio Review Stockholm (Sweden): www.spwk.eu/Portfolio-Reviews
Descubrimientos PHE (Spain):
www.phe.es/en/phe/descubrimientos
Festival Voies Off (France):
www.voies-off.com/index.php/en
Krakow Photomonth Portfolio (Poland):
Review www.photomonth.com
Emergentes DST (Portugal):
www.encontrosdaimagem.com/en

Other
Obscura Festival Portfolio Reviews (Malaysia): www.obscurafestival.com/about
Foro Internacional de Portfolios (Argentina):
www.encuentrosabiertos.com.ar/inscripcionypremios.php
CONTACT Portfolio Review (Canada):
www.scotiabankcontactphoto.com

SMALL-BUSINESS MANAGEMENT & INVOICING SOFTWARE
Blinkbid: www.blinkbid.com
Studio Cloud: www.studiocloud.com
Success Ware: www.successware.net
Shoot Q: www.shootq.com

CHAPTER 6: PHOTOGRAPHY IN THE DIGITAL AGE
WEBSITE SERVICES
Squarespace: www.squarespace.com
Photo Folio: www.aphotofolio.com
Cargo Collective: www.cargocollective.com
Wordpress: www.wordpress.org
Photo Shelter: www.photoshelter.com

GLOSSARY

art buyer: An individual who is a link between a advertising agency and freelance photographer, responsible for buying work for the agency.

art department: The group of individuals, part of a photography production, responsible for building, dressing and styling a photography set. Can consist of prop stylists, set builders and set designers.

art director: An individual responsible for overseeing the artistic direction or concept of a photo shoot.

advertising agency: A business dedicated to the creation, planning and management of a client's promotions and advertising.

budget: The amount of money a client has dedicated to a certain photo shoot. What elements fall under that budget depends on the specifics of the shoot, but it will likely include a photographer's creative fee, the location fee, the crew required to make the shoot happen, and licensing fees.

business plan: A document outlining a business's mission statement, goals, plan for reaching those goals, and time frame for achieving those goals.

carnet: A temporary "merchandise passport" for photographic equipment, used to clear customs without paying duties and import taxes.

client: The sweeping term used for the person, organization, or agency hiring you for your photography services.

commercial photography: Photography for commerce and business.

comping: The process of assembling composite images.

contract: Official document between two or more parties outlining a description of services, copyright and licensing details, payment terms and similarly pertinent details.

craft services: The department that provides food service and beverages to other departments during production.

creative director: The individual leading the efforts of the creative team responsible for conceptualizing the visual and written aspects of an advertisement or editorial.

copyright: A photographer's exclusive legal right to his or her images.

crew: The individuals involved in the production of a photo shoot, can include assistants, gaffers, digital techs, stylists.

digital tech: Responsible for managing and organizing digital workflow, image data, image back-up, processing, on set comping, image files, and hard-drive preparation.

digital workflow: The process by which images are digitally captured and then securely archived.

DSLR: A digital camera combining the optics and the mechanisms of a single-lens reflex camera with a digital imaging sensor.

editorial: A photo shoot that will appear in a magazine or print/online publication, typically fashion-based.

e-commerce: The photography of online product and catalogs.

expos: Photography events that bring together various aspects of the photography industry to showcase innovation and discuss photography-related news and topics.

estimate: Typically, a photographer or producer's breakdown of how much you will spend on a specific production, all factors considered.

first assistant: The primary photo assistant, responsible for lighting, checking camera settings, test shots, delegation and coordination, and anticipating a photographer's needs. First assistants are also entrusted to handle pre-production tasks like scouting locations and arranging second and third assets, as well as post-production tasks like returning equipment and wrapping the job.

gaffer: Responsible for the execution of the lighting plan for a production.

image-capture software: Computer software used to capture, edit, and store the digital images from a camera.

invoice: A commercial document issued by a photographer to the client, requesting payment for services rendered.

industry database: A phone and e-mail directory of creative industry professionals, e.g. Agency Access.

light-shaping tools: Used to manipulate the light or cast artificial light on a subject.

location scout: An individual responsible for the finding and securing of a location or locations to be used during a production.

medium format: A camera format that records images on media larger than 24×36mm, but smaller than 4×5 inches.

photography assistant: An individual hired to support the photographer during the shoot and acting as an extension of the photographer—anticipating his or her needs, preparing cameras, lenses, and equipment, and overseeing everything from lighting to image capture and workflow.

photo-industry consultant: An individual that offers consulting services to photographers, mainly editing portfolio and website images in addition to offering brand, marketing and career advice.

photo agent: An individual hired by a photography agency to represent photographers, helps sell their services and protect their interests.

rental house: An establishment that rents out professional photography equipment.

hard drive: A digital storage device used to store and back up images.

light meter: A device used to measure light on a photo set.

post-production: The processing and retouching of images after the completion of the shoot.

portfolio: A selection of a photographer's work, in a physical book or online.

pre-production: The work done in order to prepare for a photo shoot, including location scouting and creating shot lists.

APPENDIX | GLOSSARY

processing software: Computer software used to convert Raw images.

producer: An individual, hired by a production company, responsible for managing all the production logistics of a photo shoot, as well as the financial aspects of the production, photographer recruitment, model castings, and location scouting.

photography organizations: Groups of dedicated individuals and advocates for the photography industry and community.

photography agencies: Agencies that represent photographers, typically helping with marketing and advertising, job negotiation, and career development.

Raw files: An image file format used in professional photography to yield the highest quality images.

shot list: An outline, or storyboard, of the desired photographs to be taken during a photo shoot.

stylist: An individual hired to assist in creating the desired look on the talent.

talent: The models or actors featured in the shoot.

fixer: A local expert on the ground at a foreign location, tasked to assist with logistics at that location.

promo or promotional material: Print or online marketing and advertising materials used to promote your photography services.

SEO or Search Engine Optimization: The incorporation of search engine-friendly elements in your website to ensure it is seen by potential clients.

watermark: A faint logo or words superimposed over the top of a photograph, typically to discourage copyright infringement.

INDEX